Sufi Meditation and Contemplation

Sufi Meditation and Contemplation

Timeless Wisdom from Mughal India

Edited by Scott Kugle

Translated by Scott Kugle with Carl Ernst

Published by Sulūk Press
112 East Cary Street | Richmond, Virginia 23219
sulukpress.com

Cover image and frontispiece of Khwaja Muʿin al-Din Chishti

Cover design by Sandra Lillydahl

This edition is printed on acid-free paper.

ISBN 978-0930872-90-8

Names: Kugle, Scott, 1969– , editor, translator. | Ernst, Carl W., 1950– , translator. | Jeeli-ul-Kaleemi, Syed Mohammad Rasheed-ul-Hasan, 1932– 2013, author of preface.
Title: Sufi Meditation and Contemplation: Timeless Wisdom from Mughal India
Description: Richmond, VA: Sulūk Press, 2012. |
Includes foreword, preface, introduction, glossary, index.
Identifiers: LCCN 2011944266 | ISBN 9780930872908 (paperback)
Subjects: LCSH: Sufism | Chishtīyah BISAC: Religion/Islam/Sufi | Religion/Mysticism

Printed and bound in the United States of America

Table of Contents

Foreword

> We have sent from among you a messenger
> Recounting to you our signs
> Teaching you scripture and wisdom
> Teaching you what you never knew before
> So remember me, that I may remember you
> Be grateful to me and do not turn away.
>
> Qur'an, Surat al-Baqara 2:151-2

With these words, the Qur'an urges all who believe to remember God. We are so forgetful and distracted that we need a constant reminder to remember God. And we are often so selfish that we need some incentive, which the Qur'an in its merciful aspect gives to us: "Remember me, that I may remember you." God promises to remember us, to the extent that we remember God. Of course, God is aware of us always through the divine attributes of being creator, sustainer and nurturer; if God were not aware of us we would simply cease to exist. Yet in the endless giving of divine bounty, God is not merely aware of us but actively remembers us through the divine attributes of being the One who gives and blesses, the generous and compassionate. And in the inscrutable hints of divine wisdom, God does not merely give but promises to give at our own request. So the Qur'an says, "Remember me, that I may remember you" to convey God's promise to remember us—with all the powerful attention of the divine presence—at the instigation of our remembering God—with all the weak distraction of our wavering concentration.

With this verse, the Qur᾿an lays out an Islamic charter for meditation and contemplation, which has inspired Sufis for over a millennium. God has sent from among us a messenger in Muhammad who repeats and affirms the message that has come to us countless times: that God is one, so people should unite in belief and ethics and love around that one God's message. He recounts to us God's signs that are words of scripture in a holy book and are also insights of wisdom in our conscience.

Among these signs that teach us in our ignorance is guidance to meditate, to find the skillful means to grow closer to God's presence. This is not through acts of ritual and law, which show our dedication and obedience. This is through attitudes of yearning and self-surrender, which show our love and intimacy. Meditation and contemplation have no appointed time and no set formula. Like medicine, one takes them as one needs them, with the dosage and frequency determined by the intensity of one's illness and the stubbornness of one's constitution. Sufis have found in meditation and contemplation an antidote for self-righteousness, which is the sickness most often spread by religious institutions.

Indeed, Sufis believe that the Prophet Muhammad brought revelation that established the religion of Islam, and in that there are many blessings. But that same revelation reminds us that religion once institutionalized brings many dangerous diseases like hypocrisy, self-righteousness, fanaticism and the pious condemnation of others. Sufis believe that this same revelation also brought the cure for such diseases in the form of wisdom, self-scrutiny, humility and selflessness. The Prophet Muhammad by his own example taught the practical method to cure one's heart of such disease. Meditation is the way to instill the values in the heart, to such a depth that the heart itself is transformed. The heart then is not merely an organ in the body, and is not just one's own personal center; when properly activated through meditation, the heart opens up to reveal the very presence of God with one and with all.

To find this state of loving intimacy is the advice of the Qur᾿an when it says, "So remember me, that I may remember you." And according to Sufi teachings, to meditate and contemplate is the way to draw God down to you and to allow yourself to be lifted up towards God. But to truly remember God is to utterly forget yourself! So if, for a moment or a minute, for an hour or a lifetime, one can forget oneself in all one's conceits and lusts and wants, then one truly finds one's original state of being with God. What Sufis teach in the way of meditation is just this: to forget oneself as opposing God and to find oneself in intimacy with God. Having set foot on this path, one finds oneself to be less and less, and one finds God to be more and more, until nothing remains of the self except that which is with God and is of God. "Remember me, that I may remember you."

The word in Arabic that means "remembrance" is *zikr* (as it is in Persian and Urdu and countless other languages used by Muslims). This phrase in the Qur᾿an really means "Do my zikr," and this translation highlights that remembering God is a practice. It is something to do. One must learn to do it from one who already knows and set aside time to do it. It is a practical skill, and one must practice until perfect. It is like learning to play a musical instrument; one feels awkward or painful at first, but as it becomes habitual the awkwardness turns to beauty and the pain becomes pleasure. In this sense, Sufis have explored the practice of zikr and offered many skillful means of remembering God; these range from the subtle to the forceful, from the communal to the private, and from the abstract to the melodic. Like music that appeals to anyone whatever her or his native language, these means of zikr can appeal to any spiritual seeker regardless or his or her religion. Because this zikr is taught by Sufis who take their inspiration from Islam and Muhammad, their means of zikr is rooted in Islam and is colored by an Islamic style. But the application of this zikr is universal, as it addresses our weakness and distraction as human beings, and this distress is not limited to Muslims. Sufis urge us to learn zikr as one learns a practical art, to discover its virtues and to integrate them into one's life.

This book offers contemporary seekers some guidance to performing zikr and practicing it, as an individual or in solidarity with a community. The book presents contemporary English translations of three Sufi texts which are about meditation and contemplation, which explain why the practice is necessary, how it should be done, and what effects can be expected from its dedicated performance. All three texts come from the Mughal era in India, which witnessed a flowering of Sufism in many innovative personalities, diverse mystical orders and bold literary expressions. I am very grateful to Omega Publications and Pir Zia Inayat Khan for having given me the opportunity to edit this collection of texts and to translate some of them. I have learned much from a close reading of these texts and a discussion of their meaning with spiritual guides. I hope that through this translation, others will learn better and practice them deeper than I am able to.

I dedicate any benefit that comes from this book to two beloved Sufi guides who have lit my way: Pir Zia Inayat Khan (of the Sufi Order International) and Pir Rasheed-ul-Hasan Jeeli-ul-Kaleemi (of the Khanqah-e-Kaleemi based in Hyderabad, India).

Scott Kugle
Professor of Islamic Studies
Emory University
2011

Preface

In the name of God, the compassionate and caring One.

I am pleased that Omega Publications decided to publish this book of texts about meditation. We are all grateful to Pir Zia Inayat Khan for suggesting this project. These valuable texts in Persian belong to our common lineage, the Kalimi Sufi order, with its roots in the Chishti and Qadiri traditions.

The most detailed of these texts is *Kashkul-i Kalimi* or *The Alms Bowl of Hazrat Shaykh Kalimullah*. I first read *The Alms Bowl* when I was a student in Hyderabad, India, and read it over and over throughout my life. Hazrat Shaikh Kalimullah says that his book provides morsels that you can eat and digest according to your own taste and capacity. The most important thing for a translator to do with this book is to make it very succinct and accessible.

Shaykh Kalimullah compares his book to a beggar's bowl with which he has circled around to different spiritual teachers asking them for teachings. He would beg for teachings and he collected the pieces of this knowledge. He gathered together these teachings the way a beggar would gather together bits of food to make a meal. For this reason, Shaykh Kalimullah explains in the beginning of his book what a *kashkul* is. It is a special bowl that mendicant Sufis would use to go from house to house. The kashkul was made of a special wood that was black in color, from a type of gourd which was dried, cut in half and cured with oil so that it could keep food from getting spoiled.

In this book, entitled *Kashkul* or *The Alms Bowl*, Shaykh Kalimullah collected spiritual teachings for all people who seek the truth and are sincere in their spiritual quest. Through it, they will know the right way to seek God's presence and experience the sweetness of God's intimacy. Yet he says that each person's disposition is different. Each person has a different liking and a different taste, depending upon his constitution; what tastes good to one person is not liked by another. Shaykh Kalimullah gathered many different kinds of spiritual teachings and practices, so that there is something in it for everyone. You can chose from it the practices that suit you, and leave others aside that are not to your taste, for each person has a different capacity.

But these days, very few people read *The Alms Bowl* in India. It has never been published in an English translation, and its Urdu translation is long out of print. People from our community in Hyderabad want to get this book republished. *Inshallah,* if there is the right intention, then the means will come to get this work done and revive this book, because the Urdu translation needs to be made clearer so that common people can understand its meaning. It is heart-warming to know that Pir Zia Inayat Khan and his community can publish it in English, so that people in America and Europe can read this book.

It might happen that a translator uses certain terms in English that do not expresses the real meaning of the text. The translation should be approved by me; you may call me the servant of the Kalimi Sufi Order and the upholder of its traditions. If I review the translation then, *inshallah,* I might catch any error and recommend an appropriate correction, so that the book's true intended meaning might get expressed clearly. You cannot always translate the same word in the same way. It might be used in one place to mean one thing, and in a different context it can mean something else. A translation has to express not the words but the inner kernel of meaning so that the reader gets the message properly.

Reading this book, one sometimes finds that its words are plain but their meaning is quite obscure! It is very difficult. The translator must look beneath the words to grasp the essential meaning and then must find the right words in a new language to convey that meaning. I have read this book many times and each time I read this book I perceive new things and get new meanings from it. I discover new things each time I read it.

I first read this book under the tutelage of my father, Syed Mohammad Fakhr-ul-Hasan Kaleemi. Since my father's time, I have seen a tremendous change in the conditions of life. We used to go to the hilltop shrine of Baba Fakhr al-Din Pahari outside of Hyderabad and spend whole days there in a spiritual retreat. When I was young, we had a visit from Pir Vilayat Inayat Khan, the father of Pir Zia Inayat Khan. Pir Vilayat came from America in 1950 and stayed for a few months in Hyderabad. I was a young man then working at the State Bank of Hyderabad during the day and taking college classes at night. Pir Vilayat did not speak Urdu, and my father, Syed Mohammad Fakhr-ul-Hasan, did not speak English—so I was honored to translate for them. We belong to the same lineage and teaching as Pir Vilayat's father, Hazrat Inayat Khan. The spiritual guide of Hazrat Inayat Khan was Syed Abu Hashim Madani who lived in Hyderabad. He was a disciple of my great-grandfather, Syed Mohammad Hasan Jeeli-ul-Kaleemi.

Syed Mohammad Hasan had come to India from Medina in the early 19th century when the Mughal ruler was still in power. He was a descendant of Shaykh Abd al-Qadir Jilani and that is why our family is named Jeeli (which is the Arabic way of pronouncing Jilani). In Delhi, he took initiation in the Kalimi Sufi order. At first he shied away from joining the Chishti order because he was an ardent follower of the Qadiri order, a little like Dara Shikoh's attitude that he expresses in *The Compass of Truth*. But Syed Mohammad Hasan eventually realized that the Kalimi Sufi order was both Qadiri and Chishti in its orientation—it combined these four Sufi orders into one path, trying to take the best of each. Pir Zia Inayat Khan has written about all of this in his excellent book, *A Pearl in Wine*.

Syed Mohammad Hasan moved from Delhi to Hyderabad. He was succeeded by his son, Syed Zia-ul-Hasan Kaleemi, my grandfather who raised me like his son and gave me initiation. When Pir Vilayat came to Hyderabad, he found that my father, Syed Fakhr-ul-Hasan Kaleemi, was the head of this lineage. Pir Vilayat came to our house to learn more about the spiritual practices of the Kalimi lineage. My father told Pir Vilayat that he could give him traditional Sufi training. At first, Pir Vilayat hesitated to accept this, because he considered his father alone to be his spiritual guide. My father told him that he respected that, and would act only as his mentor and helper. He would convey to Pir Vilayat the same training that his father, Hazrat Inayat Khan, received in this Sufi order in Hyderabad long before. So Pir Vilayat Khan accepted this and my father guided him during a spiritual retreat and trained him in meditation.

For the spiritual retreat, we went to the hilltop dargah of Baba Fakhr al-Din Pahari. This is an isolated place on a hill outside of Hyderabad not far from the Astana Kalimi. This is where my father directed Pir Vilayat to go in order to find a peaceful place with no distractions. During this spiritual retreat, my father instructed him on how to hold the image of one's Pir-o-Murshid in mind while meditating. This instruction was how to achieve *fana' fi shaykh* or obliteration into the personality of one's spiritual guide. Shaykh Kalimullah explains this in *The Alms Bowl*—to meditate or pray as if it were your Pir doing it rather than you yourself.

When you do anything important, you should hold in your imagination the image of your Pir. This is called *tasawwur-i shaykh* or seeing the image of your Pir. You slowly learn to not just see his image but imagine that your Pir is with you supporting what you are doing. Finally, you understand that your Pir is actually doing it and you are not. Here is a beautiful couplet in Persian that illustrates this:

Karavan-am hama bi-guzasht ze maidan-i shuhud
ham chun naqsh-i kaff-i pa nam o nishan-am baqi-st

My caravan has departed from the realm of manifestation
I'm like a footprint left behind—all that remains is
    a name and a sign

Your Pir who has given initiation was himself initiated, and this chain of initiations leads back to the Prophet Muhammad. Ultimately absorption into the personality of your Pir leads to absorption into the personality of the Prophet as the most realized human being. This is a step towards *fana' fi'llah* or obliteration in God. Although the Prophet is a human being, he is in touch with God. He appears to be a person, but through him one encounters God's presence. He is full of divine light. These are steps on the path towards understanding and experiencing the secret of oneness of being. In Urdu we have a poem that conveys this meaning.

Muhammad sirr-i wahdat hai koi ramz un-ka kya jane
shari'at mein to banda hai haqiqat mein khuda jane

Muhammad is the secret of oneness
    His hidden meaning who can know?
In the religious law, yes, he's merely human
    His ultimate reality only God can know!

I remember when Pir Vilayat Inayat Khan went into his retreat and I was present when he came out. My father told him that now he was ready to go back to the West and take up his spiritual work.

It is important for each spiritual seeker to make time in his busy schedule to pray and meditate. This book, *The Alms Bowl,* is about how to meditate so that God remains with us always in our hearts. You might ask how can God be in our hearts? Our hearts are limited and finite. But God is like water. Water can flow everywhere. Wherever it is, water takes on the appearance and the shape of its vessel. So if you put clear water in a colored glass, it appears that the water is colored. It appears to be the same color as that glass. The water is not that color, but it appears so to us. In this way, God is in everything and permeates all things, but we don't see it properly. We see only forms and colors. A poet has expressed this in a beautiful way in Urdu:

Sanam ham dair ham but ham brahman ham
kare kis ki puja charhe kis ko chandan ham

I am the priest, I am the statue, I am the temple,
I am the idol
Whom do I worship? To whom can I offer incense
of sandal?

In Urdu we call "the idol" the thing that we desire most in the heart, such that we worship it. That is the beloved idol or *sanam*. "The temple" describes this whole world and all that is in it, full of beautiful things like a temple. "The Brahman" is the one who stays in the temple to conduct the rituals and lead people to the idol. The Brahman is a priest who worships with *puja* and spreads sandalwood paste on the statue of the idol. But the poet says that all these things are within you. You are the idol, the statue, the temple and the priest. So why should you bother to go to anyone or anywhere? There is no need. All these things are already within you, if you would just understand. If you say anything, then it is really God who says it through you. If you think anything, then it is really God who thinks it through you. This is the state of person who regards nothing in this world but God.

You see, although God created this world there is really nothing real about it except for God. In the beginning, God desired to see God's own self and enjoy. So from having this desire, God extracted from God's own divine light a certain light. This was the light of Muhammad, may God bless him and grant him peace. From this light of Muhammad, God created the entire universe: this world, the mountains, stones, trees, oceans and waters.

After making this world, God created Adam. God infused into Adam this light of Muhammad. For this reason, Muhammad is sometimes called "the light of the beginning and the light of the ending," because the light of Muhammad was before all of creation and then later was infused into Adam and his progeny, such that Muhammad was born to shine this light clearly throughout the world. For this reason, it is said that the light of Muhammad is the first and best of all creation, because it was extracted directly from God's eternal light. All light came from Muhammad's light, which was the first thing that God created. From one came two. Between the two there was recognition and attraction and love. With love, the two became three. From there the multitude of creation came into being.

There is one being that is absolute; that is God's essence. Other beings that come into being from it later are called shadow. They have no existence of their own, but are cast as forms depending upon the absolute being. Absolute being is being from and though its own self. It is conditioned by nothing else—by neither time nor space. But other beings are dependent upon something else and conditioned by other beings. You are a being. You are dependent upon your parents and conditioned by them. Without your parents, you would not have any existence. Your being has a cause and a beginning and an ending. But absolute being is not like that. It is the condition upon which all other beings depend, and it is the source of all other beings. Every other being has a source from which it comes and the source of all beings is the absolute being.

As absolute being, God's essence is unknowable. There is no sign, no sense, no indication that it exists, because there is no existence other than it. It is as if God's essence remained hidden behind a curtain of unknowability. But God's essence allowed other levels of being to emanate from it, such that the universe and this world could exist as we know it. This is so that love could be manifest. There is a very important point to understand here! God's essence is absolute being, but God wanted to see and recognize God's own being. To do this, God created the light of Muhammad from God's own divine light and made it other than God. From this light of Muhammad, God created the universe and this world. Thus there was a differentiation between the divine being of God and the lower being of the cosmos and this world. From differentiation is born love and longing.

The real lover is one who cannot think of anyone else or anything else except for his beloved. There are two kinds of passionate love. One is relative love (*ishq-i majazi*) and the other is real love (*ishq-i haqiqi*). What is relative love? It is like when I see you—you come and I am happy. I'm so happy that I leave all my other work to spend time talking with you. If you don't come back in a day or two, I get worried and restless. And when you do come, I get so happy that I forget about everything else except you.

Relative love is for a person who comes and goes. But real love is when I perceive the spirit that is in you and animates you, and I understand that this spirit is given by God. Real love is when you perceive that the tongue of the person you love is not his, but it is given by God, and that his eyes are not his, but are given by God. When you understand this, then you transcend relative love and arrive at real love. You understand that if the person you love is so wonderful, then what about God who gave everything to this person you love, which makes him lovable? When you understand that, it is so bewildering. It is wonderful. That is real love. It is God who gives all these beautiful qualities that make a person lovable, not that person himself.

Through cultivating relative love one can arrive at real love. I look at people as creatures of God—I don't see their caste, creed or sex. I see that they have everything that I have—the same eyes, the same nose, the same limbs. There is no difference. Shaykh Kalimullah writes in a philosophical language that each person is a "specific manifested being." When you read this, you should understand yourself. You are a specific manifested being. From the perspective of your being a limited being, you become a lover and thus you are drawn to your Pir-o-Murshid as a beloved. You are the lover and your Pir is your beloved. In both is the same thing—love—but it appears as manifest differentiation. That difference in appearance only confirms the unity in our essence. You and I are not two different things. There is one thing that is shared in common—that is love.

We all share in the nature of the primordial human being. We are all the same in potential, and we are only different in how much we actualize our potential to love. Shaikh Kalimullah writes in *The Alms Bowl* that "Human perfection consists of passing through the state of losing one's self in God so that one might achieve the state of remaining with God as eternal." Pay attention! He explains that all things come from and exist through the singular essence of God. Everything that is you—your heart, your mind, your eyes, everything that is yours—is really only God. God and only God. Anything you see, you are really seeing God. Anything you hear, you are really hearing God. But you need to refine your understanding to perceive this.

This is why you need to meditate, in order to refine your power of imagination. Shaikh Kalimullah explains how to do this in so many ways in *The Alms Bowl.* But the single most essential thing on the Sufi path is love. Without love, nothing you do is of any benefit. Without it, prayer is just movement, like exercise. It is not beneficial and, in fact, it could be very harmful. Love for God is expressed and demonstrated through love for other people and for all of creation.

You must burn with love like a candle. Its nature is to burn down, slowly dwindling away towards death but giving off so much light. Wherever it is, in whatever environment or surroundings, the candle gives off light. Whether in a mosque or temple, the candle burns and gives others light. That is the way you must be. When you are no longer a slave to your five senses, you perceive God in every thing, behind every phenomenon. This is expressed perfectly by Rumi in a verse that we hear sung in *qawwali*.

Khud kuza o khud khuza-gar o khud gil-i kuza, khud rind-i sabu-kash
Ta bar sar-i an kuza khareedar bar amad, bi-shikasht o ravan shud

He is the pot and he is potter, he is the clay and the drunken reveler
Reeling up to the wine-vat to buy a cup, he smashes it and disappears

God is the potter but God is also the clay. There is nothing that is separate from God. God is in nature—that is a most important thing to see. Nature must be preserved and protected, as in trees and in the environment, for all these are a phenomenon through which God manifests. They are things of beauty, and we feel awe when we appreciate them and reverence when we protect them. So we have to see in nature the manifestation of God, and worship God with increased intensity through our protection of nature.

The Sufi path consists entirely of maintaining good *adab*, meaning loving and respectful behavior. It is how you treat people and the environment and all things around you. Sufism is not about rites and rituals, customs and ceremonies. Some people think that Sufism is about having a long beard, or wearing a cloak, or putting a certain colored cap on your head. These things are not Sufism at all! They are customs. Sufism is an attitude of respect and benevolence towards all people and all things around you. It is adab, and it comes directly from the heart.

These are the basic teachings of the Kalimi lineage, of which I'm the servant. These are the teachings that Shaikh Kalimullah wrote about in *The Alms Bowl*, which combines the best of Chishti and Qadiri wisdom and also insights from other Sufi lineages. It is my honor to teach them to whoever wants to learn, despite all my faults. Some learn them here in Hyderabad, or sometimes I am invited to Delhi or to America to meet people and teach them whatever little I can. Hyderabad is my place only because my ancestors are buried here. I am merely a servant of the Astana Kalimi. Who am I? I am nobody! I am nothing but them working through me. May reading this book help to clarify things for you. But remember that no book can substitute for a spiritual guide to teach these things. May God grant both you and I the awareness of God's eternal presence, to worship with understanding and to act rightly with compassion.[1]

Syed Mohammad Rasheed-ul-Hasan Kaleemi
Hyderabad, India
2011

---

1. A fuller biography of Pir Rasheed al-Hasan Jeeli ul-Kaleemi can be found in Scott Kugle, *The Merciful Door: Living with a Sufi Master in India* (London: Beacon Books, 2022).

Translator's Introduction

This book presents three Sufi texts on meditation and contemplation. These texts explain why meditation is necessary to mysticism and to living a realized life. The texts demonstrate how it should be done, as a meditation on Islamic scriptural texts and prophetic example, and through the mediation of a Sufi guide with whom one has taken initiation. The texts also hint at what effects can be expected from its dedicated performance, in the form of medicine for various diseases of the heart, mind and spirit.

Each text is quite different in purpose and tone. Yet each text speaks to the others in a dialogue about the practice of meditation. They are intimately linked in their focus on meditation techniques that have Islamic roots but universal relevance. They are united in a concentration on the human body and how it can be refined into an apt vehicle for the performance of meditation until it virtually resonates with the presence of God.

These three texts from the Mughal era are about mysticism, and they discuss Sufi meditation techniques directly, though they emphasize the need for the mediation of a spiritual guide before one can really benefit from their spiritual medicine. In this summary, each of the five terms starting with "m" requires some elaboration. They will be discussed one by one here, as an introduction to the texts and their purpose.

Mysticism

All three texts deal with mysticism, but the term *mysticism* is notoriously difficult to define. As an abstract noun in English, *mysticism* is a relatively new term coined to mean any systematic cultivation of mystical knowledge. This is a special kind of knowledge, often called intuitive or noetic knowledge, which has the effect of breaking down the distinction between knower and object known, such that both are united in knowledge. Indeed, the cultivation of mystical knowledge breaks down any dualism whether conceived as knower and known, seeker and sought, or lover and beloved.

This mystical knowledge is not like other kinds of knowledge which can be acquired through observation, rational speculation or traditional learning. Rather it is a kind of knowledge that transforms the knower in the process of becoming known, and therefore can be conceived of as "experiential knowledge" or "wisdom." It comes to one in a flash of intuition rather than as a result of study, yet it requires rigorous preparation before one can receive it. It is not knowledge of an object, but is rather knowledge of the framework through which one knows, and is therefore called "paradigmatic knowledge." It is not knowledge of an object that is separate from the knower; rather it is knowledge of the knower's own basis in knowing. It is knowledge of what unites the knower and the object of knowledge, a unity that erases the illusion of the knower's distinctiveness. In this way, it is knowledge that challenges the basis of our egoism and potentially overcomes it.

In Persian, this mystical knowledge is called *ma'rifa,* and the systematic cultivation of it is known as *'irfan*; both these terms are derived from the Arabic verb for "to know" yet it is quite distinct from the conventional term for knowledge—*'ilm*—that can be learned through study, observation or reason. These three texts all seek to convey the urgent need of everyone for this mystical knowledge, and they each explain practical techniques to prepare oneself to receive it. All three texts assume that the reader is a sincere seeker of this mystical knowledge, is willing to undergo rigorous experiences to gain it, and has already taken initiation with a teacher who can guide one to it. Each author of these texts names his spiritual teacher and emphasizes how initiation (*bay'at*) was a necessary step in opening the way to gain awareness of this knowledge.

Readers should understand this important point. Without a spiritual guide, one can certainly read these texts and one might even learn important things from reading them. But it will be nearly impossible to practice what these texts preach if one does not have a spiritual guide to whom one is linked by initiation and to whom one can consult in practice. If one does not have a guide but sincerely desires to have one, these texts can be useful and they give specific recommendations for ways to seek a guide or substitute for this lack. For these texts all come from the tradition of Sufism (*tasawwuf*), in which mystical knowledge is conveyed through relationships. A basic premise is that one cannot experience mystical knowledge on one's own; rather, only by establishing a relationship with another can one overcome one's self-centered preoccupation and cultivate mystical knowledge. Sufis express this with the pithy saying that "If one has no spiritual guide one has the Tempter (*shaytan*) as a guide."[1] For Sufis, finding a spiritual guide is part of the search for mystical knowledge, and the difficult decision to take initiation with a guide is an act of devotion and love that is a necessary step towards embodying this knowledge.

In Sufism, mystical knowledge is not an abstraction, but rather manifests through relationships, and it begins with love for one's spiritual guide in very human form. As the Sufi

1. Annemarie Schimmel, *Mystical Dimensions of Islam* (Chapel Hill: University of North Carolina Press, 1975), 103.

poet sang, "Every community has a right way and a direction to pray... Facing the captivating face of my guide—I pray that way!"[2]

So the topic of these texts is mysticism, and in that sense they can be compared to other mystical texts from many traditions. But these are Sufi texts, and so their style of mysticism is distinct, colored by Sufism and shaped by Islam. One must appreciate their distinctiveness in this regard if one is to extract wisdom from them and engage in the practices they describe.

Meditation

These texts describe meditation practices. They explain the principles of meditation, its means and its effects. The reader may be perplexed at the very existence of such texts. It is explained above that Sufis consider having a spiritual guide to be paramount and someone whom one may learn from and consult with. So the reader is excused from wondering why, if a spiritual guide is so important, do Sufis write texts? Don't these texts speak directly to the reader, explaining mystical practices in writing, alleviating the need for a spiritual guide?

The answer to this concern is twofold. Firstly, these texts are relatively rare and they are also bold. They do aim to capture teachings in written words that are normally reserved for oral teaching from a guide to a disciple—"breast-to-breast" as it is known in Persian (*sina-ba-sina*)—when and how one's guide deems fitting. These texts themselves explain that this knowledge is usually best kept secret, but that some allowance is made for the written word to convey some of it for the

2. Amir Khusro recited this couplet "har qawm rast rahi dini o qiblah gahi...man qiblah rast kardam janib-i kaj kulahi," when his spiritual guide Nizam al-Din Awliya paraphrased Qur'an 22:66 to say, "To every community there is a religious way and a direction for prayer." An alternate story relates that his friend and fellow disciple, Amir Hasan Sijzi, recited this; see Syed Akbar Hyder, *Reliving Karbala: Martyrdom in South Asian Memory* (New York: Oxford University Press, 2006), 118–19.

benefit of sincere seekers. These texts never claim to replace an actual spiritual guide. Indeed, they presume that one already has a guide, and that one is reading the text to supplement reliance on one's guide.

Secondly, these texts should be understood to be an aid to learning about meditation rather than a sufficient source. These texts are like having a cane that can help you walk in difficult circumstances. Having a cane in your hand will do you no good if you have no feet of your own! You cannot walk with your hand, but keeping in your hand a cane can help you walk. In the same way, a text cannot teach you Sufism in place of a guide, but having a text to read can help you learn about Sufism if you do not have a guide and it can help remind you of what you learn with a guide. We often need reminding, and reading texts is a good way to refresh one's memory and retain one's focus amid the distractions of routine life.

A Sufi text is especially helpful when the topic is meditation. There are a bewildering variety of meditation techniques known to Sufis. Some of them are simple in form and some are quite complex. Some of them involve elaborate patterns of repetition or movement, and some of them require absolute stillness combined with intricate internal visualizations. These practices are designed to instill in one a serenity, bliss, insight, yearning and rapture. These are feelings that one should have during prayer, the basic Islamic ritual in which a devotee stands to face God and recites divine words. But these feelings do not always come during the external ritual, due to our innate egoism and its distractions. So Sufis have taken the basic ritual of reciting divine words and crafted meditation practices from them, to address directly the problem of egoistic impurity and selfish distraction. Zikr as meditation takes phrases from the Qur'an or names of God and crafts them into formulas that can be recited outside of ritual prayer or internally without ritual at all. These meditation formulas can be intensified by focusing on only one word or one syllable or one sound which can be internalized in one's very breathing, banishing the very distinction between inside and outside, self and other.

In this sense, Sufi practice is very similar to certain meditation practices in Hindu communities. Sacred chanting is necessary in order to properly conduct rituals from the very Vedic roots of Hindu worship. But chanting certain phrases could be taken as meditation practice itself, outside of the context of performing a ritual; such phrases are known as *mantra,* and this word has entered our English vocabulary. A mantra can be further reduced to a certain sound, called *japa*, which can be repeated in and of itself for a more intense feeling of concentration. In Mughal India, these two practices were explicitly equated, and zikr was often explained as the practice of japa.[3]

Learning about these meditation techniques is a bit like learning recipes to cook. They appear complex in explanation but become rapidly familiar when put into practice, such that writing them down is very useful for one who is just learning them. Yet a recipe's true flavor only emerges after long practice, once the written text has long been put away on the shelf and the technique that once seemed complex has been thoroughly internalized.

Mediation

Cooking may be an art, but to cook well requires love. It is love that turns mere food into a meal. It is no wonder that Muslims, even those who do not call themselves Sufis, often perform zikr or meditation while cooking, such that love and devotion might be mixed in with the ingredients. Like cooking, meditation is not merely a technique, though learning it may require some technical know-how.

---

3. Guy Beck, *Sonic Theology: Hinduism and Sacred Sound* (University of South Carolina, 1993), 135.

In Sufi meditation, techniques should never be separated from their philosophical framework and devotional basis. Without love, these meditation techniques are merely rote behaviors. The three texts presented here make very clear that as one meditates one must hold in mind the image of one's spiritual guide to invoke love, reverence and devotion. Concentrating on this image and through this image is a necessary condition for performing meditation. In this Sufi tradition, the image of one's guide (or person whom one loves deeply) is called by several different terms. It is called the medium (*wasita*) or connection (*rabita*) or meeting point (*barzakh*).

One does not meditate upon God's names or qualities or essence directly; the very nature of the human mind forbids us from such direct access to the divine presence. Rather, one calls to mind the image of one's guide as a medium, and through the love that image evokes one can begin to meditate upon God. This love then serves as a current or breeze that energizes one's meditation practice and carries one's awareness beyond routine limitations. Meditation through the image of one's spiritual guide is a skillful means to focus one's love and concentrate one's spiritual energies. One could say that meditation without mediation is mere sedation.

Medicine

The texts presented here urge us to meditate. They urge us to meditate regularly, intensely and continuously. This is because meditation is understood as a kind of medicine. It is not a sedative that makes us momentarily forget our pain, but is rather a curative that eliminates diseases which prevent us from living in tranquility. The metaphor of medicine helps us to understand these meditation practices and why the texts insist that they be practiced with and through the body.

How do we know that we are sick? We feel anxiety and fear. We experience craving and revulsion. We wake up in the middle of night in terror or we fall into despair when things do not happen as we expect. These are symptoms of our sickness, and our sickness is egoism. Afflicted with egoism, we misinterpret sensory perception as reality, react with exaggerated attachment to pain and pleasure, and allow our awareness to be distracted by objects that appear external to us and by feelings that manifest internal to us. All in all, we think of "my being" as separate from the being of others, or being in general. That is our disease. It is a disease that afflicts the heart and from there weakens our whole self.

The Qur'an depicts the heart as the very center of the human being, and it can be in different states. The person who has no faith has a heart that is hard as if rusted shut, so that it is dark. Some people's hearts are so rusted that what should shine is dull and what should move is petrified: "There is rust on their hearts because of the consequence of their deeds."[4]

A bit of rust can be polished away with a little vigorous cleaning through meditation and good deeds and repentance. But if this rust of negligence and misdeeds grows thick and hard, then it begins to affect the nature of the heart itself: "With that, your hearts then became hardened such that they are like stone or even worse in hardness."[5] In contrast, the human heart was created to be flexible and open such that it radiates with light; in all of creation only the human heart can reflect the light of God in its fullness, such that the human being can be said to be created in God's own image.[6]

The human heart is in danger of not living up to its potential and not fulfilling the goal of its creation. The heart is diseased in people who are egotistic, stubborn, stingy, cruel, cunning and hypocritical: "They only deceive themselves yet they do not perceive it—in their hearts is disease and God only increases them in their disease."[7] And so we need spiritual doctors who can diagnose the ailments of our hearts. We find such

4. Surat al-Mutaffafin 83:14.

5. Surat al-Baqara 2:74.

6. This hadith has been recorded in the collections Sahih al-Bukhari and Sahih Muslim; see Annemarie Schimmel, *Mystical Dimensions of Islam,* 188.

7. Surat al-Baqara 2:10-11.

doctors among Sufi masters who guide us to healthier ways of being. They teach us that the human heart should not accept duality, for "God has not made in the human chest two hearts but one."[8] But how can we maintain a single focus for the heart, when our human attention is pulled in myriad directions by our limited body embedded in this phenomenal world that elicits in us cravings and desires? The heart can maintain a single focus by concentrating on the one true reality, which is God. This is the remembrance of God or zikr, which is achieved through meditation and which imbues the heart with restfulness and tranquility that comes only from having a single focus, for "God lets go astray those whom God wills and God guides those who repent, those who believe and with remembrance of God find tranquility, for in remembrance of God alone do hearts find tranquility." [9]

Sufi masters are best understood as doctors. The symptoms of our existential distress are best understood as afflictions of the heart. The heart is best understood as the center of one's being where God's presence and one's person meet and mingle. And there in the heart one must maintain a singleness of focus and concentration and orientation towards God, to ignore all that is otherness and duality and falsehood and darkness. This state is known as concentration (*jam'iyat*) among the Sufis and it heals the heart of all its ailments, supports the body in all its struggles, clears the mind of all delusions, and keeps the soul pure of all defilements that obscure its intimate union with God. So meditation is the remembrance of God, and meditation is the Sufi masters' prescription for healing a broken heart.

Indeed, the tranquil heart that constantly remembers God is transformed. It becomes like a mirror which looses its own nature in the radiant image of that which it reflects. In this way, the heart that remembers God begins to realize that it

8. Surat al-Ahzab 33:4.
9. Surat al-Ra'd 13:28.

is not separate from God. In fact, the heart that remembers God is the indwelling place of God, where God manifests in this world. The Prophet Muhammad taught that God revealed that, "In the body of Adam there is a lump of flesh, and in that lump of flesh there is a secret, and in that secret am I."[10] If you want to find God, then look within. And one looks within by meditating on the presence of God, thereby clearing from one's vision everything other than God. This is the way of meditation that Sufi mystics taught.

Mughal Era

Mysticism is arguably a universal phenomenon. Wherever you find human beings you find mysticism, at least when the living conditions allow people to look within and explore the ground of their own being human. Yet mysticism takes different forms, depending upon the religious beliefs that support the cultivation of mystical knowledge. And more incisively, mystical texts are shaped by the social conditions and language of their time. As texts, they are objects that were produced in a time and place, even if the ideas they aim to convey are universal.

All three texts come from South Asia and date to the Mughal era. All three are written in Persian language, the language of court-life, high culture and literature during that era. The Mughal era lasted from 1526 until 1857 in the region of Northern India and Pakistan. This period of three centuries witnessed the expansion of a powerful dynasty that spread a rule of law and profit from commerce that united many disparate regions, brought together people from diverse ethnic and caste backgrounds, and sponsored an unprecedented dialogue between religions that were normally in conflict. The Mughal emperors, their family members and their court aristocracy largely

---

10. This is a hadith qudsi discussed in Carl Ernst and Bruce Lawrence, *Sufi Martyrs of Love: the Chishti Order in South Asia and Beyond* (New York: Palgrave Macmillan, 2002), 131–33.

saw Sufism and Islam as identical. They tried to legitimize their rule by building monuments to great Sufi teachers of the past; they sought to expand their power by imploring the blessings of Sufi guides of their era. Some of them even practiced Sufism in their devotional lives with less or more sincerity, depending upon their personal capacities and circumstances.

Under Mughal patronage, music, art, poetry and philosophy flourished with an intensity and interpenetration that was rarely seen before or after. This atmosphere nourished a flowering of Sufism in many innovative personalities, diverse mystical orders and bold literary expressions. There were Sufis who championed Islamic orthodoxy, and also Sufis who challenged the idea that Islam was the only means to salvation. There were Sufis who maintained the unique tradition of their individual orders, and also Sufis who sought to blend the different orders and emphasize their common principles. There were Sufis who embraced music as the highest means of meditation, and also Sufis who rejected music as sensuous impiety. There were Sufis who moved in the highest echelons of elite society, seeking to guide them, and also Sufis who rejected the powerful to speak up for the impoverished, living with the downtrodden. There were Sufis who explored with the subtleties of Islamic theology, and also Sufis who boldly crossed the boundary of confessional allegiance to find fellowship with those of other faiths like Hindus and Sikhs and Yogis. The three texts presented here are fruits of this era, and reflect these tensions and possibilities. Though their origin is in the Mughal era, their relevance is far beyond the limits of Mughal times.

For Muslims and Sufis today, the Mughal era is a wonderful time to hearken back to in search of inspiration and guidance. It was an era of Muslim supremacy but with a spirit of inclusivity. It was an era of great optimism for Muslims, as the Mughal emperors engineered a dynamic and expansive empire that elevated Islam in a form that could embrace people of other faiths and empower them to join its cause and reap the rewards of the peace it offered. Rajput kings joined forces with the Mughals through military alliance and marital bonds, with most Rajputs retaining their staunchly Hindu faith while others converted to become Muslims. Some Rajput Hindus like Mira Bai embraced *bhakti* mysticism that emphasized love and allowed Sufi and Hindu devotees to find common cause. Others who trace their origin to Rajput families converted to Islam and nurtured devotional music, such as those who refined Hindustani classical music and who became adepts at *qawwali* singing. Hindus who followed the ascetic path and practiced Hatha Yoga in various diverse communities seem to have entered an intimate dialogue with Sufis. Many Sufis in the Mughal era admired Yogic practices, learned them from Hindu practitioners, and found them to be congruent with Islamic teachings.

The inspiring teacher of the Sikh movement, Guru Nanak, lived during the first decades of Mughal rule, and his teachings illustrate the ecumenical spirit and optimistic mysticism that characterized this era. He taught that God was one and beyond description, but those who love God are inspired to describe God with myriad images, each of which is true yet fails to encompass God's truth. Guru Nanak had close relations with many Sufi teachers, yet he resisted assimilation into Islamic orthodox doctrines. Although the Sikh movement, as it gained strength and popular support, ran into conflict with Mughal rulers, the Sikh Gurus maintained close and intimate relations with Sufi teachers who were loyal to Mughal rule, and many verses of Sufi poetry were integrated into the Sikh holy book.

In addition, the Mughal era was a time of intense interaction between Christians and South Asians of all religions. Mughal prosperity attracted European Christians to Asia in search of merchant profits, diplomatic advantage, and missionary debate. Their travelogues indelibly shaped the European imagination of what Asia was like, and fostered a cultural familiarity which was to last even as Europeans turned from diplomacy to commerce. European art styles and Biblical illustrations began to affect Mughal miniatures, and Mughal paintings were collected by Europeans to become museum treasures. Even as European merchants evolved into colonial occupiers who would help topple the Mughal empire, the Mughal era remained a topic of fascination and admiration for European historians, and remains one of the models for a multicultural and inter-religious polity that found a way to unite people in a common cause without stripping them of their own religion, language, ethnicity and identity.

The Mughal era witnessed an unprecedented diversity of Sufi orders that interacted with the pluralist religious environment of South Asia. Reflecting this reality, there are many Sufi orders (*tariqah*) featured in the texts presented by this book. Readers should be familiar with the Sufi orders, so as to make sense of the references to them. The most popular and widespread Sufi order in South Asia is the Chishti order; its teachings were brought from Syria and Afghanistan by Muʿin al-Din Chishti when he settled at Ajmer in Rajasthan. He adapted Sufi teachings to fit into South Asian cultural norms, devotional practices and aesthetic ideals; and his followers such as Farid al-Din Ganj-i Shakar and Nizam al-Din Awliya led a florescence of Sufi thought, practice, poetry and music that deeply influenced South Asia. One text presented here is attributed to Muʿin al-Din Chishti, the founder of this order.

Despite its popularity, the Chishti order was not actually the first Sufi order to come to South Asia. It was preceded by the Suhrawardi order, which was established by Shihab al-Din ʿUmar Suhrawardi who cooperated with the Caliph in Baghdad to create a Sufi order that would spread throughout the Islamic world and unite its followers in spiritual discipline.[11] His devoted followers brought this Sufi order to many regions

11. Schimmel, *Mystical Dimensions of Islam,* 244–46.

of South Asia, where they endeavored to influence political leaders, become community leaders, and spread Islamic norms. But the Suhrawardi order's close relations to the elite actually limited its popularity. The Chishti order, which avoided the elites, enjoined voluntary poverty and embraced local culture, soon overshadowed their Suhrawardi forerunners. Suhrawardi Sufis are mentioned in these texts, but references to Chishti Sufis are much more pronounced.

The Qadiri Sufi order spread later through South Asia. It was founded by ʿAbd al-Qadir Jilani, a great preacher in Baghdad and a scholar of Islamic traditions.[12] Through his later descendants and followers, the Qadiri Sufi order spread along the sea-lanes and trade-routes in the Arabian Sea to the coasts of South Asia. By the Mughal era, the Qadiri order had reached Delhi and other cosmopolitan urban centers where, led by a series of brilliant teachers, it spread its influence widely and reached within the ruling Mughal dynasty. The author of one of the texts presented here, Dara Shikoh, was both a zealous follower of the Qadiri order and also the crown prince of the Mughal dynasty.

While the Qadiri order focused intensely on the "unity of being" and affected the intellectual elite, another Sufi order was spreading among the common soldiers and administrators of the Mughal Empire. This was the Naqshbandi order that was founded in Central Asia by Bahaʾ al-Din Naqshband. It emphasized the interiorization of Sufi practices so that the public might not know who was doing Sufi meditation in silence and through breath control. This interior focus was combined with scrupulous performance of traditional religious duties, to the point that Naqshbandi Sufis were identified as champions of Islamic orthodoxy among other Sufis in South Asia for whom Islamic belief was assumed rather than asserted. Among the Naqshbandi Sufis, meditation practices were to be subdued

12. Schimmel, *Mystical Dimensions of Islam,* 247–48.

and quiet, to the point that they advocated silent contemplation over meditation that was usually vocal, often communal, and sometimes also musical.

These four Sufi orders are considered to be the four major orders in South Asia even today. We find the Chishti, Qadiri, Naqshbandi and Suhrawardi orders mentioned in the three texts presented here, in that order of frequency. Indeed, in the Mughal era these orders were mingling: it became common for a Sufi to have taken initiation into two or more of these orders, which served to cool down the rivalry that the orders sometimes fostered among themselves. By the time of Shaykh Kalimullah, one of the authors presented here, these orders were being routinely blended. Shaykh Kalimullah received initiation into all four orders from his one spiritual guide, Shaykh Yahya Madani. He passed this blended initiation on to his own followers in the Kalimi order, who by belonging to the Kalimi order share initiation into the Chishti, Qadiri, Suhrawardi and Naqshbandi orders together.

Beside these four major orders, there were many other Sufi orders active in South Asia, representing diverse styles of mystical devotion. A relative late-comer to South Asia was the Shattari order, which was introduced from Central Asia, where it was known also the ʿIshqi order (because of its emphasis on *ʿishq* or passionate love) or the Tayfuri order (because of its reverence for Shaykh Bayazid Bistami whose personal name was Tayfur). Shaykh Kalimullah also had an initiation into the Shattari order, and though he did not emphasize it, he was influenced by Shattari techniques of meditation and contemplation. Members of the Shattari order led a flowering of Sufi creativity in devotional practices, Yogic exercises, poetry and music during the early Mughal era. As Sufis from South Asia travelled to Arab lands and to Mecca in particular, they encountered other orders like the Shadhili order. The Shadhili order was founded by Abuʾl-Hasan Ali al-Shadhili from Morocco, and it dominated the mystical life of North Africa, Egypt and Yemen. Shaykh Kalimullah, for instance, mentions this order in his text, *The Alms Bowl*, even though it was comparatively rare in South Asia; one finds links to the Shadhili order only in coastal regions where trade across the Red Sea to Arab lands flourished, such as in Gujarat.

Other Sufi orders were local to South Asia, like the Firdausi order. Its greatest spokesman was Sharaf al-Din Yahya Maneri from Bihar, whose Sufi letters with their incisive psychological insight achieved lasting and well-deserved fame. His name and teachings are quoted in the texts presented here, though by the Mughal era the Firdausi order had all but died out. There were other Sufi orders that were more diffuse and less organized, to the point that they do not really deserve to be called "orders" at all. These were Sufi movements like the Qalandars and the Malangs who opposed all formality and norms; they inhabited many Sufi sites and spaces yet they mocked all Sufi institutions and questioned the need for ritual and social order. They were "antinomian" Sufis who felt it was hypocrisy to uphold the law.

Much like modern hippies, the Qalandars believed in a simple life of owning little and desiring less in order to be free of social constraints and religious formalism. They abandoned the practice of meditation or contemplation, and sought to realize God through opposing the self-righteous and enjoying simplicity, poverty and hallucinogenic substances. They had little use for complex meditation practices such as those presented in these texts, and, perhaps in this way, to achieve the most potent form of liberation from egoism! But for the rest of us who accept social structure and retain use of our rational faculties, meditation remains a potent medicine and a useful means to realize closeness with God.

This is the starting place of all the texts presented here. They assume that the readers have a firm power of reason, through which they can seek to overcome egoistic urges. They presume a certain familiarity with Sufi orders and Islamic scriptural sources, which the readers can use as familiar guides when entering the unfamiliar interior terrain of meditation. They urge the reader to leave routine preoccupations and perceptions for a while, in order to later return to social life transformed through meditation. These texts from the Mughal era are about mysticism, and they discuss Sufi meditation techniques directly although they emphasize the need for a spiritual guide's mediation before one can really benefit from their spiritual medicine. Let us turn now to the texts themselves.

Sufi Authors in this Book

The author of the first text presented in this book is Shaykh Kalimullah. He lived in Delhi, in the heart of the Mughal city known as Shahjehanabad near the Red Fort and the Jamiʿ Masjid. He was born in 1650 and died in 1729, having lived through the high point of Mughal expansion and power.[13] He was primarily a Sufi master of the Chishti order, but also had initiations into several other orders. The eminent scholar of Sufism in India, Khaliq Ahmed Nizami, has described Shaykh Kalimullah as leading a "renaissance" of the Chishti order that enlivened the original ethical principles and mystical creativity of the early Chishti masters.[14] Shaykh Kalimullah had his primary initiation into the Chishti order, but he also received from his spiritual guide simultaneous and equal initiation into other orders: the Qadiri, Naqshbandi, Suhrawardi and Shattari orders.[15]

Shaykh Kalimullah was a Muslim intellectual and prolific author in addition to being a powerful and prominent Sufi master of his time. One of his great achievements was to "recenter" the Chishti order in Delhi, in the heart of

13. The most accessible biography of Shaykh Kalimullah is Zia Inayat Khan (ed.), *A Pearl in Wine* (New Lebanon, NY: Omega Publications, 2001), 303–6.
14. K. A. Nizami, "Chishtiyya," *Encyclopedia of Islam* (new edition, Leiden: EJ Brill, 1960-), volume 2, page 55.
15. Ernst and Lawrence, *Sufi Martyrs of Love*, 28-29.

the Mughal Empire. The Chishti order had spread widely throughout South Asia from the 14th century; as political power became dispersed among regional kingdoms, so too the Chishti order developed regional variations and local prominence, championing local languages and regional dialects. But Shaykh Kalimullah took advantage of the Mughal Empire's centralizing force, and he began to reunify the many regional Chishti centers and emphasize the core teachings of the original Chishti lineage.

Shaykh Kalimullah was aware that many practices of the Chishti order were controversial especially as the Naqshbandi order became more prominent among Mughal imperial officers and soldiers. The Naqshbandis disavowed listening to music as a form of worship, and discouraged vocal zikr as a meditation practice. In this environment, Shaykh Kalimullah wrote various books describing and defending the meditation practices of the Chishti order, and demonstrating their commonalities with meditation practices found in other orders, including the Naqshbandi order. His oral teachings were recorded in Persian by a follower of his, entitled *Majalis-i Kalimi*, and the letters he wrote to his successor were published, entitled *Maktubat-i Kalimi.* Both these books show Shaykh Kalimullah's efforts to both reassert the core practices of the Chishti order, which had enlivened Muslim faith in South Asia for so many centuries, and also to temper its practices so as to be integrated with those of other Sufi orders.

The Delhi home of Shaykh Kalimullah became a religious center: it was a *madrasa* where people came to study, a *khanqah* were they came for devotions, and it became a *dargah* when he was buried there (people still visit his tomb and pray there, though the original building was destroyed in the war of 1857). He initiated into his Sufi order both men and women, both Muslims and people of other faiths.

Shaykh Kalimullah wrote many original books to explain Sufi principles and practices. One of his most ingenious compositions is the work translated here, entitled *Kashkul-i Kalimi* or "The Alms Bowl of Shaykh Kalimullah." In it, he gives detailed instruction on how to perform various kinds of meditation and contemplation, and he explains the principles involved and their intended effects. Each practice he compares to a morsel of nourishing food that is dropped in his alms-bowl as he goes begging at the door of different Sufi guides and diverse Sufi orders. His tone of voice is much like a doctor giving prescriptions for various cures. Before him, a few Sufi guides had written explicitly on meditation practices, but none in as much technical detail and procedural clarity. Most Sufi guides were satisfied to simply note that zikr or meditation is required and beneficial, but they did not feel the need to write out detailed procedures or they felt that this knowledge was secret to be divulged only to those initiated by them. Shaykh Kalimullah was characteristically bolder. He encouraged his successor, Shaykh Nizam al-Din Awrangabadi (died 1729 in Aurangabad), to write a sequel on meditation practices that expanded his original contribution.[16]

Shaykh Kalimullah wrote many other books. His *Muraqqa'-i Kalimi* or "The Patched Cloak of Kalimullah" describes different methods of praying and making invocation. His *Tasnim-i Tawhid* or "Cups from the Font of Paradise" describes God's absolute unity and the mystical insight this gives us into the true nature of existence.[17] He wrote many

---

16. Nizam al-Din Awrangabadi, *Nizam al-Qulub,* Lithoprint in Persian (Delhi: Matba'-I Mujtaba'i Press, 1309 AH). About this text, see Ernst and Lawrence, *Sufi Martyrs of Love,* 33-34; and Kugle, *Sufis and Saints' Bodies,* 232; and Inayat Khan, *Pearl in Wine,* 306–8.

17. Kalimullah, *Tasnim al-Tawhid,* published in an anonymous English translation as *Tasmin-ul-Tauheed or The Unity of God* (Madras: Hoe and Company, 1909).

smaller books on aspects of Sufi devotion in addition to texts about medicine, astronomy and interpretation of the Qur'an.[18]

Many great Sufi leaders of the modern era trace their heritage back to Shaykh Kalimullah. Some who took it as their mission to spread the Sufi message to new frontiers were from the Kalimi order, like Hazrat Inayat Khan who left India to teach in Europe and North America, or Soofie Saheb (Haji Ghulam Muhammad Sufi Siddiqi, died in Durban) who left India to teach in South Africa. These pioneers were both inspired by the Kalimi teachers of Hyderabad, who were from the family and followers of Syed Mohammad Hasan Jeeli-ul-Kaleemi (died 1890 in Hyderabad).

The author of the second text presented in this book is Dara Shikoh. He was both a Sufi sage and a prince of the Mughal royal family. He lived in Agra and Lahore from 1615 until 1659.[19] He was the eldest son of the Emperor Shah Jehan, who named him to be the crown prince. Though born into the ruling dynasty, Dara Shikoh from an early age showed the proclivity to be an intellectual explorer and spiritual seeker. He became a Sufi disciple of Miyan Mir (died 1635) and Mulla Shah Badakhshi (died 1661), two leaders of the Qadiri order who led a Sufi revival from Lahore.[20]

Dara Shikoh represents the cosmopolitan, intellectual and spiritual currents that were strong in the Mughal era. He was an accomplished scholar and author, despite his administrative

---

18. Kalimullah, *Tilka 'Ashara Kamila,* Arabic text with Urdu translation (Delhi: Astana Book Depot, 1406 AH); and Kalimullah, *Siwa al-Sabil,* Arabic with Urdu translation (Delhi: Astana Book Depot, no date); and Kalimullah, *Ma La Budd-i Kalimi,* Arabic with Urdu translation (Delhi: Astana Book Depot, no date). His other works are listed in Inayat Khan, *Pearl in Wine,* 305.

19. Josef Meri (ed.), "Dara Shikoh," *Medieval Islamic Civilization: An Encyclopedia*, vol. 1, page 194-5; and Schimmel, *Mystical Dimensions of Islam*, 360–62.

20. See Aziz Ahmad, *Studies in Islamic Culture in the Indian Environment* (Oxford: Clarendon Press, 1964), 191–200.

and military responsibilities as the crown prince and governor of several provinces. By the age of 25, he had authored *Ship of the Saints* (*Safinat al-Awliya*) on the lives of great Sufi masters of the past, both male and female. Then two years later, after having taken initiation into the Qadiri order and having tasted the fruit of meditation under the guidance of his teacher, Mulla Shah Badakhshi, Dara Shikoh wrote another book about his spiritual experiences; this was entitled *Deliverance of the Saints* (*Sakinat al-Awliya*) on the teachings, miracles and spiritual states of his own Sufi guides in the Qadiri order. This he wrote only after he had "been ennobled by having taken initiation, engaged in mystical practices and became knowledgeable about the stations of the Sufi way."[21]

In the next decade of his life, Dara Shikoh had immersed himself in Sufi meditation and also studied Hinduism through texts and spiritual guides. In particular, he made a deep study of the Upanishads and had an intimate familiarity with bhakti teachings. He had recorded a session of question-and-answer between himself and a Yoga adept named Baba Lal Das (known also as Babalal Vairagi), and also wrote a Persian treatise arguing for the complementarity and continuity between Islam (as understood through Sufism) and Hinduism (as understood through Vedanta), entitled *Majma' al-Bahrain* or "The Meeting of Two Seas."[22] He further had this treatise translated into Sanskrit (entitled *Samudra Sangam*) so that it might be read and appreciated by Hindu scholars.

Dara Shikoh wrote a further text about Sufi approaches to meditation, entitled *Risala-i Haqq-Numa* or "The Compass of Truth" which is translated in this book. In this book he discusses Sufi meditation as practiced by the Qadiri order in South

---

21. Dara Shikoh writes this passage and more biographical information in the introduction to *The Compass of Truth*, as translated in this book.

22. Published as Muhammad Dara Shikuh, *Commingling of Two Oceans: Majma' ul-Bahrain*, trans. M. Mahfuz-ul-Haq (Delhi: Hope India Publications, 2006).

Asia, and he explains the cosmological framework in which these meditation techniques were practiced. Though his sources were distinctively Qadiri, the cosmological scheme that he offers (of different subtle realms that are beyond and within the material world and sensory perception) is largely shared by all Sufi orders. But Dara Shikoh is particularly bold about describing these realms in prose, and explaining how meditation techniques, if practiced with rigor and zeal, can take the spiritual seeker through them.

Dara Shikoh was a bold and even audacious spiritual explorer, and he courageously upheld the equality of Muslims and non-Muslims in his era. But he was not a successful ruler. One historian of Mughal administration calls him "a mediocre general and an insensitive leader" despite his intellectual gifts and religious insights.[23] When his father, the Emperor Shah Jehan, fell suddenly ill in 1657, a war of succession broke out between the Emperor's four sons, all mature men with impressive capabilities. In this war, the third youngest son Aurangzeb won. He had forged a strong military power base as the governor of the Deccan province. When he won the war of succession at Agra and Delhi, Aurangzeb had Dara Shikoh and his son executed in 1659, and kept his ailing father in prison. Aurangzeb imprisoned one of his remaining two brothers while he defeated the other in battle.

Aurangzeb ruled with an iron fist until his death in 1707. Aurangzeb continued to show symbolic deference to long-dead Sufi guides and patronized some of their tombs, as was the tradition of Mughal rulers. But he never sought advice from living Sufi guides or kept intimate company with them, as had his rival brother Dara Shikoh. The luster of the Qadiri order that Dara Shikoh had favored dimmed in the aftermath of this succession battle, and later the Qadiri order often merged in

23. John Richards, *The Mughal Empire* (Cambridge University Press, 1993), 152.

practice with the Chishti order. Aurangzeb oversaw the external expansion of Mughal rule, though from within the empire grew weak, setting the stage for Shaykh Kalimullah's life and work. Shaykh Kalimullah sought to give advice to the later Mughal rulers even as their power declined, and he strove to recenter the Chishti order (now merged with the Qadiri and other orders) in Delhi to bolster the spiritual courage of its leaders and citizens, as detailed above.

The author of the third text presented in this book is Mu'in al-Din Chishti, who established the Chishti order in South Asia. At least, we can say that the text is attributed to Mu'in al-Din Chishti, though its real author remains anonymous (if the text can be said to have a single author!). The text attributed to a respected ancient source—Mu'in al-Din Chishti (died 1236 at Ajmer Sharif in Rajasthan)—is most likely a later written record of oral teachings that evolved in practice over many generations. The earliest manuscripts that we find of this text date to the 17th century. Therefore, it is safest to date this text to the Mughal era, during which bold authors wrote down ideals of an evolving Sufi tradition that may have been passed on in earlier generations as oral teachings.

It may be possible that these oral teachings have their origin in the words of Mu'in al-Din Chishti, though they were written down only in the Mughal era, at least three centuries after his death. Sufis of the Mughal era attributed this text to Mu'in al-Din Chishti, the most highly revered Sufi master of that era and empire. Mughal rule was firmly established by Emperor Akbar, who established the tradition of imperial deference to this founder of the Chishti order. Emperor Akbar attributed the long awaited birth of a son to the blessings of a Sufi guide, Salim Chishti (whose humble tomb at Sikri, outside of Agra, was transformed by Akbar into an elegant mausoleum surrounded by the grand mosque of his new imperial capital, Fatehpur). In gratitude, Akbar started the royal tradition of pilgrimage to Ajmer to pay respects to Muʿin al-Din Chishti, and he also patronized grand building projects at this tomb and the tomb of Nizam al-Din Awliya at Delhi.

Under Mughal patronage, Muʿin al-Din became known as *Sultan-i Hind*, "Ruler of India," or *Hind al-Wali*, "Spiritual Governor of India." At the height of the Mughal empire, the princess Jehanara, the sister of Dara Shikoh, could make a pilgrimage to Ajmer and write sincerely, "With my own hand I put the highest quality of attar on the perfumed tomb of that revered one, and having taken off the rose scarf that I had on my head, I placed it on top of the blessed tomb... If I had the choice, I would always have stayed in the sanctuary of that revered one, which is the marvelous corner of security."[24]

Many Sufis assert that such a renowned personality must have left written texts conveying his spiritual teachings. Yet his immediate successors, like Nizam al-Din Awliya, noted that none of the Chishti leaders before him ever wrote books. By the advent of the Mughal era, there were texts in circulation that were attributed to Muʿin al-Din. There is a *Divan*, or collection of poetry, that is written in his name; some of the Persian ghazals in this collection may be his words, but the whole collection is surely not his work or else Nizam al-Din Awliya would not have said that none before him had written books.[25] There was also a book purporting to be the verbatim record of Muʿin al-Din's teachings, as faithfully recorded by his friend and followers, Qutb al-Din Bakhtiyar Kaki; similarly, there is a book that purports to be Muʿin al-Din's own record of the oral discourses of his spiritual guide, Haji

---

24. Ernst and Lawrence, *Sufi Martyrs of Love,* 89 quoted from *Anis al-Arwah* or The Confidant of Spirits, in the account of her pilgrimage to Ajmer appended to her Persian biography of Muʿin al-Din Chishti written in 1643; as found in Qamar Jenah Begam, *Princess Jehan Ara Begam, Her Life and Works* (Karachi: S. M. Hamid 'Ali, 1991), 117-23.

25. *Divan-i Hazrat Muʿin al-Din* (Kanpur: Munshi Naval Kishor Press, no date).

ʿUthman Harwani (known also as Osman Haruni). Yet these books must have been written later and "retrospectively attributed" to these spiritual luminaries, for we know that the first book of oral discourses of any Chishti leader was the innovative *Fawaʾid al-Fuʾad* or *Morals for the Heart,* which recorded the words of Nizam al-Din Awliya almost a century after the death of Muʿin al-Din.[26]

This does not mean that these texts are forgeries or fakes. They may indeed contain some oral teachings of these early Chishti masters that were faithfully remembered and handed down in oral tradition. But as written documents, they cannot claim to be from the era or environment of the Sufis to whom they are popularly attributed; they are certainly not the verbatim record of these Sufis, as they are often claimed to be.

The same problem confronts the reader of the small treatise attributed to Muʿin al-Din Chishti, the *Risala-i Wujud* or *Treatise on the Human Body*, which is presented in this book. It is known by many titles, and the text varies widely from manuscript to manuscript. These are signs that it is the product of oral transmission. Yet the fact the Mughal era scribes who were copying out this text seemed to not be familiar with some of its terms and images is a hint that, despite its questionable attribution to Muʿin al-Din, it may contain teachings of an archaic nature. It may contain ideas or images that do in fact date back to the time of Muʿin al-Din Chishti. When he moved from Afghanistan and Persia and settled in South Asia, he was reputed to have interacted with Brahmins and learned something of Hindu teachings and devotional music of temples.

In a similar vein, this small treatise contains teachings about Yoga and includes reference to several Sanskrit terms of ancient usage. The text is about meditation techniques and urges its readers to turn inward in spiritual discipline and introspection.

---

26. The felicitous term "retrospective attribution" comes from Ernst and Lawrence, *Sufi Martyrs of Love,* 228.

Its words may not be from the pen of Muʿin al-Din, but its ideas and images may reflect his dialogue with Indian spiritual traditions and his attempt to harmonize them with Islam, as seen through a Sufi lens. Whether or not it can be authentically attributed to Muʿin al-Din, this treatise explains some basic ideas which later Sufis in India, like Dara Shikoh and Shaykh Kalimullah, took for granted. In this sense, it is part of the Chishti tradition even if it is not authored by Muʿin al-Din, the founder of that tradition.

The Texts in Translation

This introduction may have taxed its readers' patience. In the Sufi tradition, it is said that those who really know do not speak, and those who speak do not really know. This long-winded introduction has already proved the ignorance of its author. Yet it is hoped that the readers might forgive and indulge, for the introduction might provide some readers with necessary background about Sufi mysticism and Sufis' practice of meditation in the Mughal era. It has also given necessary biographical information about the authors of the text presented here.

Now the readers are invited to turn to the texts themselves, as presented in new English translations based on the Persian originals. Before each of the three texts, there will be a brief discussion of the published and manuscript copies that form the basis of the translation, and some notes about the challenges of translation itself. After the texts, readers can find a glossary of Arabic and Persian terms that are used in the texts, for the three texts share a common vocabulary.

The Alms Bowl of Shaykh Kalimullah

Translator's Notes

by Scott Kugle

This is the most important and widely read text by Shaykh Kalimullah Shahjehanabadi, at least in the eyes of practicing Sufis. It is an indispensable manual for how to practice Sufi meditation and contemplation, complete with detailed instructions and theoretical framework. The author draws upon a wide eclectic array of sources and styles, reflecting the whole diversity of Sufi orders that were active in South Asia and Arab lands during his lifetime in the 17th century.

The playful title that Shaykh Kalimullah chose for this text reflects his concern to be eclectic and all-inclusive. He calls it *Kashkul* which in Persian and Urdu means an alms bowl of a particular type common in South Asia. It is crafted from a species of large gourd whose shell is sliced in half to create a large, heavy, sturdy oval bowl of utterly elegant simplicity. It is polished with oil to give it a characteristic black sheen and makes it easy to clean. A Sufi with a kashkul is a distinctive sight, and without having to ask for anything the alms bowl itself signals to people that he will accept a morsel in donation. One can still see a kashkul in use in places like Hyderabad, though they are becoming heirlooms of the past now, as mendicancy and ascetic renunciation become more rare (perhaps as a function of generosity becoming a rarer quality even as prosperity increases!).

Shaykh Kalimullah calls his collection of meditation techniques an alms bowl, because he circled from teacher to teacher and order to order, begging for the choicest teachings. He collected them in one text, as nourishment for the soul of the spiritual seeker. Indeed, each subsection of his book is called a "morsel" while smaller points of clarification are called "crumbs." In the introduction, he explains why he gathered these meditation techniques into one text, like food donations in a beggar's bowl. "Let this be nourishment for any who longs for the taste of sweet union with the divine. Each morsel in it has a particular quality that might be relished by some while appearing unappetizing to others. Each crumb of its bread has a special taste that some might find appealing while others consider it bland. Therefore each and every crumb is given to the seeker who is mastering this Sufi path towards the truth (that all may choose) daily bread as they prefer—whether buttered or honeyed, whether of crispy bran or hearty barley." Shaykh Kalimullah wrote this text in two months, finishing on 3 October 1690 CE (the last day of Dhu'l-Hijja 1101 AH), as he explains in the text itself. The original text is in Persian, but it has been translated into Urdu because it is in constant use by modern Sufis in South Asia.

This translation has been rendered from what appears to be the earliest printed edition, an undated lithograph print from a press that was active around the end of the 19th century and into the early 20th century. In preparing this translation, I also referred occasionally to a later undated (later 20th century) version that republished the Persian text with an Urdu translation; this was republished under the auspices of Muhammad Mustahsin Sahib Faruqi, the hereditary custodian (*sajjada-nashin*) of Shaykh Kalimullah's dargah in Delhi. He endeavored to have all of Shaykh Kalimullah's books republished with Urdu translations, in order to reach a wider modern audience in South Asia. This English translation continues the tradition by rendering the text into English in a style that, it is hoped, will be accurate, accessible and appealing to a modern audience both in the West and in South Asia.

The Alms Bowl of Shaykh Kalimullah Shahjehanabadi

In the name of God, the compassionate and merciful.

All praise be to God—from God, to God and for God alone. Blessings from God (be upon the Prophet Muhammad) and the peace of God. This is an Alms Bowl (*kashkul*) full of spiritual morsels. They strengthen the divine quality (*latifa rabbaniya*) inherent in every person and nourish the universal intellect (*nafs-i natiqa*) that animates each soul. These morsels fill the outer form of religion (*islam*) with the inner spirit of true faith (*iman*). They confer on each realized person the profound blessing of eternal life and treat with compassionate healing those who are sick with egoistic desires.

These are a few pages—no, a few chapters in reality—filled with cooked morsels comprising all kinds of meditation and contemplation. I, Kalimullah, the writer of these pages, have begged for these morsels from many spiritual teachers and guides for the sake of all who hunger with sincere appetite and truth-seeking imagination. Let this be nourishment for any who long for the taste of sweet union with the divine. Each morsel in it has a particular quality that might be relished by some while appearing unappetizing to others. Each crumb of its bread has a special taste that some might find appealing while others consider it bland. Therefore each and every crumb is given to the seeker who is mastering this Sufi path towards the truth [that all may choose] daily bread as they prefer—whether buttered or honeyed, whether of crispy bran or hearty barley. Let all seekers find something nourishing here according to their capacity. Let all with spiritual appetite (*zauq*) find here a taste of felicity.

Before this, I had written a text entitled *The Patched Cloak* (*Muraqqa'*), in which I stitched together devotions and prayers, so that those naked in the cold winter of witnessing might wrap their exposed bodies in the protective clothing of piety and God-consciousness (*taqwa*). Then at the request of some sincere friends, the writer began to collect these morsels fit for beggars starting on August 6, 1690 (1 Dhu'l-Qa'da 1101). I present them now in *The Alms Bowl* so that those with spiritual taste and divine longing might reach their full capacity. May they repay this favor with a simple wish that God grant this nobody well-being. We ask God to always ask God for nothing but God! By the grace of him (Muhammad) whom God appointed as the first of divine emanations and chose as God's own Prophet.

This book consists of an introduction, two chapters, and a conclusion. Then with all its faults, we can call it complete.

Introduction

You should know that absolute being (*wujud-i mutlaq*) was hidden and unknowable before its coming into duality (*ma'iyat*) with the material universe that is like its shadow. From that primordial unknowability there was no sign by which it could be known. As required by overpowering, absolute being—of itself by itself—exerted its potential to unfold in emanations (*maratib*) of divinity and cosmos as higher levels to lower levels. Through this duality, lover and beloved became manifest, since each manifestation generates a higher and a lower. From the perspective of being a limited manifestation, it is "lover"; from the perspective of being a higher manifestation above it, it is "beloved." The perfection of each specific manifested being (*ta'ayyun*) is in returning to its original state of absolute being. Its ultimate goal is to revert to that undifferentiated state (*be-rangi*) from whence it originated.

When I speak here of "manifestation" I mean specifically the primordial human being (*hazrat-i insan*) who is the being in whom all qualities of God's essence and divine attributes appear. In comparison to all other manifestations, the human being excels by bearing the trust (*amanat*).[1] Human perfection therefore consists of passing through the state of losing one's self in God (*fana' fi'llah*) so that one might achieve the state of remaining with God (*baqa' bi'llah*) as eternal. To realize this, one first journeys to reach God (*sayr ila'lah*) and then one journeys in God (*sayr fi'llah*). There is an end to the first journey, but in the second journey there is no end.

Morsel 1

Union is a term signifying separation from all that is other than God and indifference to all that is the world. It means focusing entirely on the divine and becoming effaced in utterly undifferentiated being and absolute oneness (*itlaq*). The initial experience of this is unselfconsciousness (*be-khudi*) and absence from all sensory perception; this is a condition resembling death, except that in death there is no presence while this state is nothing but pure presence. When a seeker experiences this, the term *wilayat* applies to him (and he is considered a "Friend of God") even if the experience lasts only an hour. Then if the seeker returns to his senses, he is considered amongst those firm saints (*ashab-i tamkin*), and this steadfastness is sometimes bestowed quickly and other times only after a long while. If the seeker remains in that state of unselfconsciousness and intoxication, he is considered one of the masters of transforming spiritual states (*arbab-i talwin*). Therefore, seekers should keep their vision focused on losing one's self and bearing witness to the divine essence of undifferentiated quality, for their spiritual

1. Surat al-Ahzab 33:72 tells that God offered "the trust" to the heavens and the mountains but they all declined in fear of bearing it, yet the human being accepted the trust, thereby becoming God's vice-regent in the world.

journey will be more perfect that way. But if the seekers' vision should stray to the right or left in order to engage other limited manifestations (*kashf-i ta'ayyunat*), they will go astray from the straight path.

Morsel 2

In writings about the spiritual path, one sees each station (*maqam*) described with a special quality and in an attractive poetic language, such that one's heart desires to experience that station alone and no other station. One feels a strong aspiration to achieve that station and exerts all efforts to get there, find no rest without it, thinking perhaps that "asking for everything means getting nothing." One thus hesitates with doubt, thinking "which station should I strive for?" or asserting "I already got that station!" Yet each station is a good choice and is worthy of the highest sacrifice.

Yet in the opinion of this humble writer it is better that seekers, instead of striving after a certain station, should focus their whole concentration on one simple goal. That is, after making their obligatory prayers (*farz*) and optional prayers (*sunna*) as the Prophet taught, along with other duties incumbent on a Muslim, seekers should resolve to stay engaged in meditation (*zikr*) and contemplation (*fikr*) and intimacy (*uns*). Sometimes, seekers might stay engrossed in offering copious devotions (*nafila*), reciting the Qur'an, glorifying God's name, chanting litanies (*wird*) and invocations (*da'wat*) and meditations (*azkar*) which all confer spiritual reward; yet seekers should leave aside inventive discourses and fanciful allusions and all other kinds of good deeds. In this way, day in and day out, seekers should obliterate the imagined existence of their ego selves, until the divine—by grace (*inayat*) granted before time—might draw them up out of their limited selves and lead them through obliteration of passing away (*fana' al-fana'*) and from there into eternal remaining (*baqa' al-baqa'*). At that point, the seeker's essence is seen as divine essence, the seeker's quality appears as divine quality, the seeker's effect is found to be divine effect, and the seeker's act is considered the divine act. Whatever leads to this consummation should be encouraged, and whatever distracts from it should be avoided.

All the various Sufi orders (*silsila*) are in agreement on this point, that the seekers of God must necessarily become so engrossed that they are removed from their own self-concern. I find that nothing leads one to self-effacement better than meditation and contemplation. Yet some Sufi orders consider certain types of meditation to be better than other types; in this alone did various Sufi masters differ.

Morsel 3

In the discourse of Sufi masters, descriptions of the ways of meditation and contemplation are numerous and varied. But most dependable is the description given by al-Sulami.[2] He says, "There are many types of meditation. One type is meditation of the tongue (*lisan*), and it needs no further explanation, as one repeats vocally a name of God or a phrase. Another type is meditation of the heart (*qalb*), which means purifying the heart of selfish desires and fiendish temptations in order that it remember God in truth. A third type is meditation of the inner heart (*sirr*), which fills the inner heart such that momentary stray thoughts which give rise to desires have no way to fix themselves in the heart. Meditation of the inner heart is the outcome of meditation of the heart. The inner heart is a subtle energy within and beyond the heart. Perpetual presence with the divine is possible for the inner heart to achieve, whereas the heart itself undergoes constant change, motion and transformation (*taqallub*) from one moment to the next, and therefore perpetual presence is not available to or through it. A fourth type is meditation of the spirit (*ruh*), which consists of the one meditating becoming obliterated and oblivious to any personal qualities of the self, when he realizes that the object of

2. Abu Abd al-Rahman al-Sulami was a great early Sufi and was one of the first to write about Sufi theory and practice in prose; he lived in Persia and died in 1021. See Schimmel, *Mystical Dimensions of Islam*, 85-87.

meditation—God—is actually thinking of the one meditating. In this state, nothing remains of the one meditating—no meditation, no spiritual state, and no personal quality. In order to understand this, one could say that God is the one meditating and remembering you before you have ever started to meditate to remember God. You can grasp this meaning through a poetic couplet:

> Considering your existence, it is strange that I'm existing
> When you begin to speak, it's fitting that I stop speaking

Then regarding contemplation al-Sulami states, "Similarly, means of contemplation are of several types. One type is the seeker's deep reflection (*tafakkur*) on all his or her sinful deeds, oppositional attitudes and weak shortcomings when performing the duties owed to God. Another type of contemplation is the seeker's reflection on God's bounty and grace and the seeker's acknowledging lack of proper gratitude for these blessings; for even if one gave thanks and showed gratitude, it would fall short of proper response. A third type of contemplation is the seeker's reflection on all that was apportioned for them before that time (*azal*) wherein one's destiny was sealed—for it is said "Dried is the pen in writing out what will happen good or bad"—and on how undeserving they are of any blessings granted to them before they ever existed. Another type of contemplation is reflection on the excellent craftsmanship and fine skill of divine design in forging all things in the material world (*mulk*) and spiritual world (*malakut*) which bedazzle the mind with God's majesty, refresh the heart's awe regarding God's greatness, and keep one aware of remembering God's presence.

Al-Sulami further explains that the object of reflection in contemplation is the self (*nafs*) while the object of remembrance in meditation is God; for this reason, spiritual leaders consider meditation to be superior to contemplation. In elaborating on what al-Sulami states, we can see that meditative remembrance (*zikr*) is an attribute of God while contemplative thinking is not. So a human act which echoes an attribute of God is more perfect, while a human act that does not echo any attribute of God is lesser. The person who meditates turns towards the divine essence, for meditation is the result of spiritual knowledge (*ma'rifat*) and devotional love (*muhabbat)*. In contrast, the person who contemplates dwells on the self, its condition, its states, its being less or more, its being too much or too little—all in all, contemplation is keeping account of one's own self (*muhasibat-i nafs*). In conclusion, meditation is in accord with contemplation, and also contemplation is in accord with meditation. But meditation is more complete, more lofty and more pure than contemplation; for contemplation on the self leads one towards repentance, while meditation on God leads one towards divine union (*wusul*). God says, "Therefore remember me for I remember you."[3] God attributes to the divine self that quality of meditative remembrance rather than the quality of intellectual contemplation.

Morsel 4

The spiritual master Shaykh 'Abd al-Karim al-Jili who lived in Zabid, in Yemen, says that the sign of one who has attained the practice of meditation of the heart is that he or she hears the sound of his or her meditation emanating from all things or from some things, either at certain times or at almost all times, depending upon the facility and capability of the one meditating.[4] He also says that the sign of one who aims to practice meditation of the spirit is that she or he hears all things glorifying God (*tasbih*) each in its own special way and beholds no agent other than God.

---

3. Surat al-Baqara 2:152.
4. 'Abd al-Karim al-Jili was a master in the Qadiri Sufi order. He traveled in India and lived in Yemen, where he died in 1403 AH. He wrote many books explaining the mystical teachings of Ibn 'Arabi, and his most famous work is *The Complete Human Being on Mystical Knowledge of the Ends and Origins* (*al-Insan al-Kamil fi Ma'rifat al-Awakhir wa'l-Awa'il*).

Ahmad Ibn Ghilan Makki says that meditation of the heart sets right the relationship between God's presence and humanity's presence. He says that meditation of the spirit lets God's presence dominate the presence of humanity. He says that meditation of the inner heart (*sirr*) leads to a state in which there is no presence of humanity but only God's presence alone. Lastly, he says that meditation of the inner essence (*khafi)* unfolds the latency of being from within the potentiality of spirit just as the entire cosmos lies latent within the inner heart.

Morsel 5

Meditation is remembrance as opposed to forgetfulness. So whatever makes you remember and stay connected with your object (God) counts as meditation and constitutes an act of worship (*'ibadat*), regardless of whether the means of meditation be a name, ritual or action performed with the body or in the body or in abstraction from the body or in any other way. Likewise, whatever makes you forget and neglect your object (God) is misguided and vain, regardless of whether the means of forgetting be a name, person, thing or anything else. For Sufis, everything said, everything done and everything felt can be meditation, on condition that it leads them to remember God and stay awake and aware. Anything which does not promote remembering is forgetfulness and should be shunned, as conveyed in this couplet:

> If I am with you, my daily work is prayer
> And without you, my prayer is merely work

Morsel 6

Spiritual masters say that meditation is of many different types. There is meditation with the tongue with words spoken out loud or recited silently. There is meditation of the heart and meditation of the inner heart. Then there is meditation of the inner essence of the heart (*khafi*), meditation of the most secret inner essence (*akhfa*), and finally meditation of the utmost secret inner essence (*akhfa'-i akhfa*).

As for meditation with the tongue, it is meditation involving spoken words in which there are syllables and letters, in a set order with some preceding and some following. If the sound of reciting these words is performed out loud it is called "vocal meditation" (*bi'l-jahr*). But if it is done silently then it is called "concealed meditation" (*bi-khufiya*).

As for meditation with the heart, it consists of reciting a word or retaining in the heart the presence of a word or name, with regard to its meaning and signification rather than to its letters and syllables. In fact, the presence of the word or name is invoked all at once including all its letters, syllables and sounds.

As for meditation of the spirit, it consists of disregarding the word or name in order to dwell in the presence of the one denoted or named [God]. This experience varies according to the capacity of the one meditating: some realize the divine presence at some times while most times being devoid of it, while some realize it most of the time and some realize it always continuously. Yet all of them are conscious that "I am one who meditates, and that during a particular time I am meditating, and that I hold a particular object as the goal of my meditation, an object which was present before my awareness (*basirat*) but which is now faded."

The furthest extreme of this kind of meditation, known as meditation of the inner heart, occurs when both the meditation and the one meditating are together effaced and nothing remains to be known or understood except the presence of the object of meditation (*mazkur*, meaning God). At this point, even the delight experienced in meditation is effaced, and there remains no awareness of any delight to be experienced. This can be called meditation of the inner essence of the heart. Similar to this station is meditation of the most secret inner essence and the utmost secret inner essence. Further discussion of these states of meditation mentioned here will come later.

Morsel 7

Shaykh Sharaf al-Din Yahya Maneri says that meditation is practiced in one of four conditions.[5] First, it could be that the tongue is busy reciting but the heart is distracted searching in the mine of other meanings. Second, it could be that the tongue is busy reciting and the heart is accompanying it to the extent that the heart is sometimes reciting but sometimes is distracted while the tongue keeps busy. Third, it could be that there is harmony between the tongue and the heart in the recitation, but sometimes the heart and tongue together are both distracted. Fourth, it could be that the tongue gets distracted and is at rest, but the heart is engaged in reciting meditations and is fully aware. This is the furthest station of spiritual development in which one's work is complete and meets the requirement of full presence and continual awareness. This is the real essence of meditation. Achieving it, the one meditating hears the voice of his or her own heart which nobody else can hear. This is what Shaykh Sharaf al-Din has said.

Morsel 8

Some spiritual masters say that novices improve their spiritual condition by performing meditation, while more experienced disciples improve by reciting the Qur'an and advanced Sufis improve by making devotional prayers (*nafil*). But in my humble opinion, it is better for a seeker to keep doing silent

---

5. Sharaf al-Din Ahmad ibn Yahya Maneri was a master in the Firdausi Sufi Order, and he died in Bihar (near Patna in North India) in 1381. The cave where he used to meditate in the Ragjir hills is still a popular place of pilgrimage. He met Shaykh Nizam al-Din Awliya in Delhi. Sharaf al-Din Maneri is most famous for his collection of letters of spiritual guidance; see Paul Jackson (trans.), *The Hundred Letters of Sharafuddin Maneri* (Mahwah, NJ: Paulist Press, 1980).

meditation. In this way, the seeker can rid the mind of the imprint of anything other than God, to assert the absolute oneness of God and turn towards God seeking presence (*huzur*) and intimacy (*uns*). The seeker should seek effacement (*fana'*) and obliteration in the holy divine presence. Realizing the truth of God means embracing the experience of being annihilated (*tams*) and erased (*tals*). This path is the quickest way to gain closeness to God and the surest way to achieve union. I acknowledge that in the process, many types of worship might be left undone. But no fear about this need be entertained, since the benefit of losing self-consciousness in this way will overshadow all omissions and deficiencies!

Morsel 9

I will now discuss some points about the proper way to engage in meditation. As stated in the book *Minhaj al-Salik ila Ashraf al-Masalik* (*The Spiritual Seeker's Method to Reach the Noblest of Goals*), there are twenty rules that guide one in meditation. Some of these rules apply to before meditating, some apply to during meditation and some apply to after meditation.

In preparing for meditation, there are five rules to follow. One must first make repentance for any wrongdoing (*tawba*). One must be in a condition of tranquility and in a state of cleanliness as if making ablution for prayer. One must concentrate on one's spiritual master for help (*istimdad*), and one must have firm knowledge (*'ilm*) that asking for help from one's spiritual teacher is in reality asking for help from the Prophet himself, may peace be upon him, that is, help from God the almighty.

During meditation, there are twelve rules that apply to the process. One should sit cross-legged or kneeling as in prayer (*salat*). One should place both hands on the knees. One should purify the atmosphere with fragrance or incense. One should wear only clean clothes. One should keep the room dark. One should keep one's eyes closed and keep the openings to one's ears stopped up. One should mentally picture the face or form of one's own spiritual master, for this is the most important rule of all. In addition, one should be absolutely truthful (*sidq*) and sincere (*ikhlas*), both inwardly and outwardly; in this context truthfulness means not exaggerating the extent of one's own effort and sincerity means not performing with hypocrisy so that others see you and hear you. One should choose words that express God's unique oneness, specifically, the saying *la ilaha illa 'llah* or "No God but God" for reciting in meditation. Finally, when reciting this saying, one must feel at all times the meaning of words in order to negate every vain imagined thing from the open expanse of divine presence and to concentrate on the only really existing thing (God). It is my humble opinion that this last rule is absolutely necessary and of vital importance if meditation is to be effective.

After meditation is completed, there are three rules to follow. One should maintain silence for some time after meditation. One should practice suspending the breath (as discussed in detail in Morsel 12). One should avoid the use of cold things like water or exposure to cool air, for these might dissipate the heat in the heart that is built up by meditation.

This is the guidance written in the book *Minhaj al-Salik.* The book further announces some benefits of meditation. Meditating by repeating the phrase *la ilaha illa'llah* (*kalima-i tawhid*), generates intimacy with God's holy presence.[6] Anyone who does extensive amounts of meditation but

6. The Sufi meditation on the phrase "No god but God" is similar in function to the Yogic practice of *pranava* or repetition in each breath of the syllable *Aum.* Beck, *Sonic Theology: Hinduism and Sacred Sound,* 86, notes that Patanjali's *Yoga Sutra* says "The sacred word (*om*) connotes him (*Isvara* or God); its repetition and the understanding of its meaning should be done." The earliest commentary on the *Yoga Sutra* is by Vyasa, who writes about this verse, "The Yogi who has come to know well the relation between word and meaning must constantly repeat it, and habituate the mind to the manifestation therein of its meaning. The constant repetition is to be of the pranava (*A U M*) and the habitual mental manifestation is to be what it signifies, Isvara. The mind of the Yogi who constantly repeats pranava and habituates the mind to the constant manifestation of the idea it carries, becomes one-pointed."

does not feel an expanded intimacy with God is doing it in vain; perhaps such a person has become slack in certain rules and must start afresh. Shaykh Ibn ʿAtaʾullah al-Shadhili has written that when a person recites *la ilaha illa ʾllah* the throne of God begins to vibrate, for the very source of these words is the realm of divine might (*jabarut*), so that the person who recites them is no longer related to the material world (*mulk*) and the realities of this world, but rather is drawn upward rising towards the realm of the spiritual world (*malakut*).[7]

There are many other benefits to reciting this in meditation. If one repeats it a thousand times every morning after ablutions, one will be able to easily secure the means of sustenance, and I feel that the word sustenance (*rizq*) is used in a general sense encompassing both livelihood of body and vitality of spirit. If one recites it a thousand times before retiring to bed, one's spirit will rest below the divine throne during the night and grow in strength. If one recites it a thousand times at noon, the force of temptation (*shaytan*) that is within will be broken. If one recites it a thousand times near the advent of the new moon, God will protect one from every kind of illness. If one recites it a thousand times on entering a town or leaving it, God will protect one from dangers and things which make one fear and grieve. If one recites it a thousand times with one's full presence and firm concentration and then sends it against an adversary who is oppressive and overweening, the adversary will be defused and negated. If one recites it a thousand times with the intention to gain spiritual disclosure of unseen things (*kashf-i ghuyub*), all secrets of the material and spiritual worlds will be revealed. Anyone who repeats it seventy-thousand times, will be ushered by God into paradise.

---

7. Ibn ʿAtaʾullah al-Iskandari is a famous Sufi master in the Shadhili Sufi order. He died in Alexandria in 1309. He wrote many valuable texts on Sufism, including *The Key to Salvation* (*Miftah al-Falah wa Misbah al-Arwah*) which is one of the earliest Sufi texts on meditation techniques. It is probably to this text that Shaykh Kalimullah refers here. See Mary Ann Koury Danner (trans.), *The Key to Salvation* (Cambridge: Islamic Texts Society, 1996).

Morsel 10

Some masters of spiritual knowledge say that meditation of the tongue leads one to the further stage of meditation of the heart. Without a doubt, when the tongue and the heart operate in union the meditation will be arranged to perfection. This arrangement is generally acknowledged by all the Sufi orders. The exception to this is the Naqshbandi order, which teaches that meditation of the heart suffices if it is coupled with internal longing (*jazb-i batin*). This is the practice they prescribe for beginners in the Naqshbandi order, conveying their teaching in this couplet:

We begin at the ending place to which others aspire
Where we end is the place that can fulfill any desire

That is their teaching, but it is clear that what is attained by experienced practitioners of all other orders is not attained by beginning practitioners of the Naqshbandi order. It is merely that giving priority to meditation of the heart is the practice advocated by the Naqshbandi order. There will surely be a big difference between the effect of a beginner practicing meditation of the heart with inner longing (*zikr-i qalb-i majzub*) in the Naqshbandi order and the effect of an experienced member of another order practicing meditation of the heart with inner longing!

Morsel 11

Some Muslim jurists reject meditation of the heart and limit the legality of meditation only to that of the tongue. This is merely a contention of their conceit. Don't they realize that meditation is remembrance and thus includes anything that is opposed to forgetfulness, which is essentially an attribute of the heart? Oh dear, don't they see that each individual has particular rules that are arranged in a way suitable to his or her own special needs?

Morsel 12

When practiced during meditation, suspension of breath (*habs-i nafas*) is considered by some to be a powerful means to eradicate stray thoughts and mental wandering. Some even consider it to be the essential means. In many Sufi orders like the Chishti, Kubrawi, Shattari and Qadiri orders, it is practiced as the primary basis of meditation. In contrast, the Naqshbandi order does not require it yet does not deny its worth. Teachers of the Suhrawardi order, on the other hand, require their followers to avoid the suspension of breath; this is the point of view of Shaykh Baha' al-Din 'Umar and Zain al-Din al-Khawafi who are both renowned leaders of the Suhrawardi order, may they both be blessed.[8] I humbly submit that there are in fact two different ways of treating the breath in meditation. One is suspension of breath and the other is restraining of breath (*hasr-i nafas*).

Suspension of breath can be done in two ways, with emptying and with filling. Suspending the breath with emptying (*takhliya*) is a technique of drawing up the breath from the abdomen while pulling the navel and the area around it back towards the spine and then suspending the breath in the chest or, according to some, to the seat of the mind (*dimagh*). While doing this, there is no need to close the nostrils, ears and eyes with the fingers, although some do this as a precautionary measure. Stopping up the nostrils, ears and eyes was a measure that originated when this practice was done while in the midst of a reservoir and submerged under water. This practice was taught to 'Abd al-Khaliq Ghujdawani by Khizr, and

8. Zain al-Din al-Khawafi was an important master in the Suhrawardi Sufi order; he died in Herat (in Afghanistan) in 1435 and wrote a text entitled *Mir'at al-Talibin* (Mirror of Seekers). See H. T. Norris, "*The Mir'at al-Talibin* by Zain al-Din al-Khawafi," *Bulletin of the School of Oriental and African Studies* 53/1 (1990): 57-63. The reference to "Baha' al-Din 'Umar" must refer to Shaykh Baha' al-Din Zakariya who established the Suhrawardi Sufi Order in South Asia; he died in 1263 in Multan (in Pakistan).

it considered extremely effective.[9] It generates an enormous amount of internal heat in the body. Sufi masters have adopted this method of suspending the breath and other methods of breath control from the Yogis and their followers, who are the perfect exponents of this craft.[10]

The second way of suspending the breath during meditation is with filling (*tamliya*). This means drawing the breath into the belly and suspending it there while making the belly swell full. By means of swelling the abdomen like this, the navel is pushed out as far away from the spine as possible. This way of breathing aids digestion of food exceedingly well.

In contrast, restraining the breath refers to taking breaths smaller than normal. It is done by cutting down the size of breath on both sides (while inhaling and also exhaling). One simply takes breaths of smaller than normal amounts. Without a doubt is generates an internal heat in the heart, yet less intense than the heat generated by suspending the breath.

The description of heat and cool above refer to the quality of the breath (once it enters the body through the bloodstream) that is called "circulating." But in addition, there is the air which is "stationary" which does not have the quality of heat or cold and therefore does not require the heart to change its condition. This remains undisturbed during both suspending and restraining the breath. If one perceives and makes it a fulcrum for the meditation, one will be doing the meditation perpetually and feel the divine presence for an extended period of time, as long as the divine extends aid for one to feel it.

During the days when one is practicing suspension of breath, one should avoid foods that are extremely moist and

---

9. 'Abd al-Khaliq Ghujdawani was an important master who founded the principles that are practiced by the Naqshbandi Sufi Order; he lived in the town of Ghujdawan near Bukhara (in Uzbekistan) and died in 1220; his name is sometimes recorded as Ghijduwani. He advocated silent zikr and consciousness of the breath according to the Persian saying "*hosh dar dam*" (consciousness in each breath). It is related that he met Khizr, the figure of eternal wisdom, and learned secrets of zikr techniques directly from him.

10. Beck, *Sonic Theology*, 206 writes that "Sufism in India accepted the ancient Hindu doctrine that speech-sound is generated by the interaction of heat (internal fire) and air (breath) in the human body."

foods that are sour. One should refrain from foods that are very heat-increasing, for they may cause illness or make it more severe. In the initial stages of this practice, it may be that blood comes out from the ears, nostrils or anus, but the seeker should fearlessly continue the practice, for the bleeding will very soon stop. One should never strain or practice suspension of breath too intensely, but increase the intensity gradually, for what seems difficult later proves light.

When exhaling, one should release the breath gently through the nostrils and not through the mouth, lest the outflow of air damage the gums and teeth. As a firm rule, one should never practice suspending the breath when on a full stomach or when hungry, but rather in a state between the two. This rule guides one in the initial stages, but for one who is well advanced there is no such rule and he may practice suspension of breath whenever he chooses.

Morsel 13

Some spiritual masters explain that people behold spiritual truths when their inner selves are cleansed and purified of attachment to sensory perception and attraction to sensual habits. Then they are filled from within by absorption in meditation and the blessing of having an internal relationship (*nisbat*) and attachment (*rabt*) with spiritual forces. This relationship causes their hearts to be illumined. In this state, the human being beholds the divine essence through this illumination, and becomes aware of what the divine wills and commands. Further, the light reflecting from the heart to the eye enables them to behold the unseen worlds with the senses of their bodies. They are then said to be drawn away completely from this world both inwardly and outwardly.

Morsel 14

The first station of the spiritual path is repentance (*tawba*) and its final stage is bewilderment (*hayrat*)—though some claim that the final station is not bewilderment but rather contentment (*riza'*) and acceptance (*taslim*). There are two kinds of bewilderment, one of which is bad and the other of which is good. The difference can be explained as follows.

The beauty and perfection of the divine essence is such that it calls for bewilderment rather than mere doubt. But sometimes there is ambiguity here, and it provokes a state between bewilderment and doubt. It should be known that bewildered wonder at some object comes from a person's knowing and perceiving the essence of that object, in contrast to doubt which comes from a person's ignorance and misunderstanding. So bewilderment comes from a person's presence with a thing while doubt comes from a person's absence from that thing. A bewildered person ascends, with each passing moment, upward towards the pinnacle of knowing something because of his passionate desire to know that thing. In contrast, the doubtful person descends, with each passing moment, down into ignorance about the reality of a thing because of his lack of attention to it.

Further, it is said that bewilderment is a compound of two things, namely knowledge of the thing's existence and ignorance of its nature. In contrast, doubt is a state of hesitation between knowledge and ignorance. One who doubts cannot be characterized as having decisive knowledge that is experientially confirmed and also cannot be characterized as having ignorance that is decisively established; rather, one who doubts has uncertain knowledge and also unsure ignorance. Such a person's deeds always oscillate between denial and affirmation. This kind of doubt is known as bad bewilderment in contrast to the good bewilderment that was described before. It is said that bad bewilderment is experienced by common people but good bewilderment is the portion of the spiritually gifted.

Morsel 15

Light becomes manifest (to the seeker) which is sometimes white, sometimes green, sometimes red and, last of all, sometimes black. This light is called light of the realm of divine might (*nur-i jabarut*). The appended diagram explains the signification of light at different places. The sincere seeker must never feel despair or delight on account of the manifestation of any of these lights!

Direction of Light	Form	Name	Signification
Near the right shoulder		*Katib-i yamin*	Angel recording good deeds
At a distance to the right		*Nur-i Shaykh*	Light of the Master
Before or in front		*Nur-i Muhammad Rasul Allah*	Light of Muhammad Messenger of God
Behind or above		*Mala' ka-i Hifza*	Light of the Guardian Angels
Near the left shoulder		*Katib-i yasar*	Angel recording bad deeds
At a distance to the left			Temptation of Satan
	Form or shape to the left		Temptation of Satan
On all sides			Temptation, if one feels fear or terror and then when it dissipates one feels no presence
On all sides			Light of God, if one feels a presence while it is there, and feels yearning when it is gone
Before chest or navel			Temptation
Before the heart			Light of the Heart's Purity

Morsel 16

Sufi masters disagree about whether the one with spiritual knowledge should perpetually bear witness to spiritual realities or not. Some say that this witnessing should be perpetual and continuous, while others say that it should not be. One spiritual master has said, "The spiritual adepts witness in a way between revealed and obscured." The reality is that the connection between the heart and the head, once it is firmly established, gets confirmed by experienced training and then never vanishes after that, though it may be that illuminations and visionary witnessing may come and may go. This is the meaning of the Arabic proverb that says, "The present moment is as swift as a sword and brilliant as lightning."

Morsel 17

In states of self-absence, unselfconsciousness, effacement and obliteration, a spiritual condition is achieved that is very subtle. That condition is impossible to describe and that place is utterly other. You might say it is nothing but the unitary totality of God (*ahadiyat-i haqq*) and absolute being of divinity. But it could be countered that, "Absolute being of divinity can never ever be conceived, for only those things can be conceived by the mind which are temporal and ephemeral. Mental forms are part and parcel of the phenomenal world, and every existing phenomenon is temporal and ephemeral. What is temporal and ephemeral cannot be absolute being, for the latter is eternal and imperishable, and what is eternal and imperishable can never be grasped by the senses." I would reply, "It may be as you say, but when seekers are in that state of effacement (*fana'*), they cease to have a self and experience no self-concern and are completely unaffected by relationality (*nisbat*) which engenders dualism—dualism of distinction between subject and object. This state is called obliteration of obliteration (*fana' al-fana'*). That is a state characterized by "nothing to know" more than "knowing nothing."

This is the very state that Abu Bakr al-Siddiq [the first Caliph] referred to when he said, "The only real knowledge is knowing you can never really know." So then how can we speak of God by saying expressions like "witnessing the essence" or "manifestation of the essence" or "loving the essence" or "knowledge of the essence" and "knowing God"? I would answer that real spiritual knowledge (*ʿirfan*) results in putting each thing in its proper place and giving each thing its rightful due. Concerning this matter before us, there are two things to consider. One is essence in its pure simplicity, and the other consists of any matter that comes after it and from it. Now, the rightful due of the first matter [about the divine essence] is that it must be affirmed, and the rightful due of the second matter is that it must be denied. True knowledge of the first is that it can never be known, while true knowledge of the second is that it can be known for what it is. One intending to know the former while denying the latter will never achieve the knowledge intended.

It is clearly known that affirming what is true is true, while affirming what is untrue is untrue. Yet not knowing about a thing does not necessitate not being able to experience its existence. In this way, we can say that the holy essence of God most exalted is something affirmed and experienced but never known. Now "witnessing the essence" means being absent from all things that are after and from the essence [meaning all phenomena]. And "manifestation of the essence" means that all phenomenal things are concealed from one's perception. The cessation of desire for all phenomenal things is the meaning of "loving the essence." Finally, ignoring all such phenomenal things is the meaning of "knowledge of the essence." In this way, you can understand the various meanings of any description of God's essence. It cannot be imagined that one can have knowledge of God directly, yet one can have knowledge of God's names (*asma*ʾ) and qualities (*sifat)* and actions (*afʿal*). These aspects of God's nature can be known, not in their actual nature but rather only in the aspect that is apparent. This is because a thing's real essence is unknowable because the real essence of all things is the reality of God, since God is the reality of all realities. Thus the reality of God's essential nature is unknowable by human beings, angels, and jinn.

The essential reality of all things is truly unknowable. To grasp this is the utmost extent of spiritual knowledge. How well someone said it like this, "The simplest of common people is just like the most select of the elite, and the first stage of the ignorant is the last stage of the learned." But still the poem holds true that reads—*Behold, what a long way it is to travel from here to there!*

Morsel 18

The system comprising these various ways of devotional exercise (*shughl)*, meditative remembrance (*zikr*) and contemplative reflection (*fikr*) consists of technical methods which must be learned. But whether they are successful depends upon the aspiration of the disciple who uses them, and having a high aspiration entails no learning or exertion. The spiritual master simply directs the disciple to empty the self by following the path of the *Shariʿa*, and then the master directs his concentration upon the disciple to offer spiritual aid, being present with the disciple at all times even when far away. In this way, the master opens many doorways for an in-pouring of spiritual energy for the disciple. This way, however simple, is rare. Many selfish people search for this simple way. Because the labors of the Sufi path and its demands are too difficult for them, they long for this simple and direct way.

Morsel 19

There is a saying that "He who has no master has the Tempter as his master."[11] In accord with this saying, every

11. This saying is popularly attributed to Shaykh Bayazid Bistami: "*Man laysa lahu al-shaykha fa-shaykhuhu al-shaytanu.*"

sincere person ought to have a spiritual guide (*shaykh*). But the question is how and where to find him. As a beginning, the seeker may not be able to distinguish between a good and a bad person, and may not know the difference between a saint (*wali*) and a common person. By mere rational analysis, he may think a bad person to be good and a good person to be bad, and thereby stumble into doubt. Shaykh Sharaf al-Din Yahya Maneri helps the seeker out of this difficulty when he says that God has not, does not, and will not allow the world to remain without saints for any period whatsoever, in all their ranks from spiritual guides to ascetic (*zahid*) to worshippers (*'abid*) to support (*watad*) to pious ones (*khayr*) to delegates (*najib*) to pure-hearted ones (*naqib*) to the interchangeable ones (*abdal*) to the axial saints (*qutb*) and the succor of the world (*ghawth*), in addition to all the various friends of God, such as those who appear mad with longing (*majzub*) and those drowned in divine love (*'ashiq*) and those beloved of God (*ma'shuq*). Therefore, the seeker must find those spiritual guides who are on this path and have these qualities. The seeker must frequent them and their assemblies. Every time on leaving the company of a spiritual master, the seeker should examine his heart to inquire whether or not it has improved by leaving aside the temptations and pollutions and all kinds of selfish thoughts that previously assaulted his heart. Perhaps in some meeting with the spiritual master the seeker felt liberated from the incessant changes in the state of the heart or experienced salvation from his former state. If the seeker observes that his heart has improved, he should stay with the spiritual guide in whose company he has experienced this good fortune, in hopes that his heart will find continuing liberation by meeting him again and again. And if the seeker observes no change in his heart, he should know that his destiny lies not with this spiritual guide and he should seek the cure of his heart at the doorstep of some other spiritual guide without denouncing or blaming anyone.

Morsel 20

Shaykh ʿAbd al-Qadir Jilani says that everyone who desires to find a spiritual master should do the following.[12] The seeker should rise from sleep at midnight, and after ablutions make two cycles of prayer (*rakaʿat*) and read as much of the Qurʾan as he can between them. He should then prostrate to God and seek salvation from God, and pray for a spiritual guide in the following way, so that God might open for the doorway of reaching him. He should pray that God will lead one of God's friends to show him the path so that God may guide him to the divine presence. The seeker should perform this prayer time and time again until it comes to fruition. The following is the prayer: "Oh my Lord, lead me to one of your intimate servants that he may guide me to you and teach me the way to reach you."[13] In addition, some later Sufi masters of the Shadhili community state that by making constant and continuous benedictions upon the Prophet Muhammad (*salawat*) along with praises to God (*tahlil*), one can find a perfect spiritual guide. They say that their guide in this practice is Imam Hasan, the son of ʿAli ibn Abu Talib (the first Imam of the Shiʿa and the fourth Caliph of the Sunnis).[14]

Chapter 1: On Methods of Meditation

Morsel 1

When a seeker finds a perfected spiritual guide and decides to take up the spiritual path, he must take initiation. His spiritual

12. ʿAbd al-Qadir Jilani (or Gilani) is an influential master from Iran who is the founder of the Qadiri Sufi Order; he died in Baghdad in 1166.

13. In Arabic, this prayer is: *"Ya Rabbi, dullani ʿala ʿabdin min ʿibadika al-muqarribina hatta yadullani ʿalayka wa yuʿallimani tariq al-wusuli ilayka."*

14. The Shadhili Sufi community was founded in North Africa by Abuʾl-Hasan al-Shadhili who lived in Morocco and Tusinia, and died in Egypt on 1258. He was a descendant of Imam Hasan. The Shadhili community spread to Mecca and Medina, and it is most likely that Shaykh Kalimullah encountered their teachings when he went to Medina to stay with his spiritual guide, Shaykh Yahya Madani, though he did not take any formal initiation into the Shadhili order.

guide will direct him to undergo a fast for three days, continuously if he can endure it, or else he can break it with an occasional slight refreshment. During this fast, the seeker is directed to repeat a thousand times the praise of God (*tahlil*), seeking forgiveness of God (*istighfar*) and invoking benedictions on the Prophet (*salat*). After the third day of fasting, the seeker should make full ablutions with a bath (*ghusul*) and appear before his spiritual guide. His spiritual guide will recite from the Qur'an Surat al-Fatiha and Surat al-Ikhlas, then the verses from Surat al-Baqara and Surat Al 'Imran and the verses of seeking forgiveness (*istighfar*).[15]

After this the master says, "Are you my disciple, and the disciple of my teacher, and of the spiritual guides of my master all the way back to the Prophet Muhammad and from him to God, the Lord of might? Do you vow to conduct your body on the straight path of the Shari'a and to keep your heart in the love of God?" The seeker answers, "I agree and promise to be led by the Shari'a and to love God," while the master places his right hand in the right hand of the seeker, according to verses of Qur'an that say God's hand is over their hands.[16] As the seeker makes this vow, all present hold the hem of his garment. If the assembly is very crowded, everyone holds the hem of the garment of those in front of them who are holding the garment of the seeker, to maintain a connection one to the other. The

15. Sura al-Baqara 2:285 *Amana 'l-rasulu bi-ma unzila ilayhi min-rabbi-hi wa'l-mu'minuna kullun amana bi-'llahi wa mala'ikati-hi wa kutubi-hi wa rusuli-hi la nufarriqu bayna ahadin min rusuli-hi wa qalu sami'na wa-ata'na ghufranaka rabba-na wa ilayka 'l-masiru.* "The messenger believes in what has been revealed to him from his Lord, and so do the believers. All of them have faith in God and God's angels and books and messengers, saying 'We make no difference between any of God's messengers.' And they say, 'We hear and obey, Oh Lord, to win your forgiveness and you are the end of the journey.'" Surat al 'Imran 3:18 *Shahida allahu annahu la ilaha illa huwa wa'l-mala'ikatu wa-ulu'l-'ilmi qa'iman bi 'l-qisti la ilaha illa huwa 'l-'azizu 'l-hakimu.* "God bears witness that there is no God but he, and so do the angels and those endued with knowledge who stand firm with justice. There is no god but God, the mighty One, the wise One."

16. Surat al-Fath 48:10.

spiritual guide then clothes the initiate with a robe (*khirqa*), saying, "The garb of piety is most excellent and a blissful end awaits the righteous."[17] Then the spiritual guide talks to the seeker in private and imparts to him a meditation according to his capability, such that none other should hear them.

A Crumb of Morsel 1

The procedure of imparting a meditation to the seeker is like this. The spiritual guide says the words of the meditation to the seeker once and the seeker listens intently. The seeker repeats the meditation while the spiritual guide listens. They repeat this procedure three times. Then the master says, "As I received this meditation from my spiritual masters so I give it unto you." The seeker acknowledges that he accepts it and will practice it. Further, he is instructed after each of the five canonical prayers to recite praise upon the Prophet (*darud*) and Surat al-Ikhlas ten times each, and to make six cycles of prayer (*rak*ʿ*at*) while saying three times "peace be upon you" (*salam*), which is called *Salat-i Awabin,* and to also perform two additional cycles of prayer to strengthen his faith, as I have stated in my book *The Patched Cloak of Kalimullah* (*Muraqqa*ʿ*-i Kalimi*).[18] And before going to bed, the seeker is instructed to repeat one hundred times "No god but God" (*tahlil*) and Surat al-Fatiha for the benefit of the souls of all his spiritual guides in his Sufi lineage.

Another Crumb of Morsel 1

Performing meditation should come before contemplation (*muraqaba*). However, some spiritual guides say that contemplation

17. The spiritual guide says *Hadha libasu* ʾ*l-taqwa wa dhalika khayrun wa*ʿ*f-*ʿ*aqibatu li*ʾ*l-muttqina,* which echoes Surat al-Aʿraf 7:26 which reads, *libasu* ʾ*l-taqwa dhalika khayrun...* "O children of Adam, we have indeed sent down to you clothing to cover your shame and for beauty, and the clothing of piety that is best."

18. *Salat al-awabin* is a prayer beyond the canonical prayers (*nafil*) that is performed after sunset prayer (*maghrib*) and consists of six to twenty cycles of prostration (*raka*ʿ*at*). It is recommended to offer peace (*salam*) after every two cycles.

is better and should come first. This is also acceptable, provided that the seeker shows the capacity for it. It is true that the greater the challenge, the greater the results. In reality, it is best to begin with meditation which is of many varieties and moods, to make the seeker stir with love and cry out with longing. After that, the seeker can pursue contemplation which leads to singularity of vision and consciousness devoid of conditions to make the seeker be still in silence.

As for meditation, there are many ways and methods. If the spiritual guide sees that the seeker is distracted by worldly aspirations, he should teach him the meditation of "negation and affirmation" (*nafy o isbat*, based on saying *la ilaha illa ʾllah* "there is no god but God"). If the spiritual guide finds a seeker with a little love for the beloved, he should teach him a method of meditation based on the name of God (*ism-i jalal*, based on saying Allah). If the spiritual guide feels that his seeker is of gentle nature and with no attachment to the world, he should teach him meditation of "divine essence" (based on saying *hu*). In short, for every kind of seeker there is an appropriate kind of meditation with an effective style and meaning. In this chapter, I will detail each kind of meditation, if God wills. My intention is not to inflate the number of methods of meditation and contemplation, as is done in some Sufi books, such that meditations add up to a thousand and contemplations run into the hundreds. No! Rather, my intention is to show you the kinds of meditation that capture the essence of the practice and the types of contemplation that encapsulate the best of their kind. Thus if anyone masters these contemplations and meditations, he may master all others.

Morsel 2

This is the method of performing "meditation of negation and affirmation" (*zikr-i nafy o isbat*) that involves pronouncing the words "no god but God" (*la ilaha illa ʾllah*) in four beats (*chahar zarbi*). It is practiced either aloud or inaudibly. One should sit cross-legged in a narrow dark room. Now, sitting cross-legged is a position connoting arrogance and pride and it is undoubtedly forbidden at all times, with the exception of sitting alone to meditate. In Islamic law, it is considered an innovation (*bid'at*). Yet it is reported that the Prophet Muhammad, upon him be peace, upon finishing his dawn prayers, used to sit cross-legged in the same place in order to do meditation until the sun shown brightly.

So one should sit cross-legged with the back straight, the eyes closed, and the hands resting on the thighs. One then uses the big toe and the next toe of the right foot to firmly grip the sciatic nerve (*rag-i kimas*) that runs behind the left knee. Putting pressure on this will produce enough warmth in the heart to generate a purity (*tasfiya*). This warmth will melt and remove the fat that surrounds and constricts the heart, which is known as the dwelling place of the tempter (*khannas*).[19] This will reduce the temptations and pollutions that plague the heart. Taking up this position, one should perform the meditation with single-minded heart and with assertive voice, either saying the words aloud or keeping silent as is suitable to one's situation and disposition.

While performing this meditation, one should observe the conditions laid down in this poetic couplet:

Medium, essence, attributes, drawing out, intensifying,
below and above
Show the spiritual seekers in each and every breath
a taste of love

Barzakh o zat o sifat o madd o shadd o taht o fauq
Mi-numayad taliban ra kulli nafas zauq o shauq

---

19. *Khannas* is the "whispering tempter" that the Qur'an asserts dwells in the breast of every person (Surat al-Nas 114:4). According to Shaykh Nizam al-Din Awliya, Khannas is the son of Iblis (Satan) who lives in the breast of all people and tries to influence their hearts; see Scott Kugle, *Sufis and Saints' Bodies* (Chapel Hill: UNC Press, 2007), 38–9.

In the context of this meditation, the terms listed in the couplet mean the following. The "medium" (*barzakh*) means one's spiritual guide's face or form. The "essence" (*zat*) refers to the divine essence of the absolute being, may it be glorified and exalted. The "attributes" (*sifat*) refer to the seven primal qualities of the divine—namely life (*hayat*), knowledge (*'ilm*), power (*qudra*), will (*irada*), hearing (*sam'*), sight (*basar*), and speech (*kalam*). "Drawing out" (*madd*) refers to prolonging the pronunciation of the first "a" in *la ilaha* or "no god." "Intensifying" (*shadd*) refers to accentuating the first syllable "i" when saying *illa 'llah* or "but God." "Below" (*taht*) refers to pronouncing *la ilaha* beginning by facing down towards the left knee and then raising the head up towards the right shoulder. Finally, "above" (*fauq*) means pausing for a while holding the breath before pronouncing *illa 'llah* or "but God" from above down onto the heart with great force.

Morsel 3

To understand the meaning of the above-mentioned method of meditation, one should know that there are four kinds of thoughts (*khatrat*). There are tempting thoughts (*shaytani*) which cause feelings of pride, anger, enmity, envy and other destructive emotions. Then there are egoistic thoughts (*nafsani*) which cause feeling of craving for food, sexual pleasure, accumulation of wealth, love of display and other such selfish emotions. Then there are angelic thoughts (*malaki*) which cause devotion, worship and other such acts which accrue spiritual reward. Finally, there are divine thoughts (*rahmani*) which cause virtues like sincerity, love, longing and other positive emotions.

So when one performs this meditation and begins facing the left knee, this is to negate satanic thoughts since the left is the abode of the tempter. Saying this, one moves to face the right knee to negate the lusts of the ego, which reside in the right lower body, for the ego and Satan mutually oppose each other and the ego is tempted to stray. The right shoulder is the abode of angelic thoughts, for the angelic scribe who writes all good deeds is there and called "the recorder of the right" (*katib-i yamini*).[20] Finally, the area of the heart is the abode of divine thoughts.

To try to hold all these concepts in mind at one time causes hesitation and confusion, so therefore they are taught within the simple process of performing this meditation (in four beats) which encompasses all these regions and spiritual realities. At the outset one should be instructed to say *la ilaha illa 'llah* in the sense of there is "no god but God." Then the meditation should be performed with the understanding that there is "no object of worship but God" (*la ma'bud illa 'llah*). Then it should be performed with the understanding that there is "no goal but God" (*la maqsud illa 'llah*). Then it should be performed with the understanding that there is "no desire but God" (*la matlub illa 'llah*). Finally, it should be performed with the understanding that there is "no being but God" (*la mawjud illa 'llah*). By doing this meditation in this ascending order, all kinds of thoughts and feelings will vanish and disappear. This humble writer suggests that a new learner can start with the very last meaning to lighten the load and to cut short the way to achieve the goal. If the learner does not know Arabic, one can teach this meditation with equivalent words in any language that he knows.

Morsel 4

This meditation can be performed in just two beats (*zikr-i do-zarbi*) with each breath. In this way, one says the same words, but the first phrase "no god" (*la ilaha*) is recited towards the right shoulder in one beat. Then the second phrase "but God" (*illa 'llah*) is recited towards the heart in the second beat. After the third or fifth or seventh or ninth repetition of

20. Surat al-Infitar 82:10-11 refers to the "honorable scribes" (*katibin karimin*) that are angels appointed to record one's good and bad deeds and preserve them for judgment day.

this, one should say "Muhammad is the Messenger of God" (*Muhammadun rasulu 'llahi*). Except for being slightly simpler, this method of meditation differs very little from the meditation on the same words to four beats, as detailed above.

Morsel 5

After performing "meditation of negation and affirmation" (*zikr-i nafy o isbat*), one should always perform "meditation of affirmation alone" (*zikr-i isbat*). Thus after meditation by pronouncing "no god but God" (*la ilaha illa 'llah*) one meditates by pronouncing "but God" alone *(illa 'llah*). After that, one should meditate on the name of God alone (Allah). The word "God" (Allah) is pronounced in a louder and more intense voice than "but God" (*illa 'llah*). And the phrase "but God" (*illa 'llah*) should be done in a louder voice than "no god but God" (*la ilaha illa 'llah*).

Morsel 6

This is how to perform the "meditation of babbling" (*zikr-i laqlaqa*).[21] This meditation consists of pronouncing the name of God (Allah) continuously without any gap or separation in an almost inaudible repetition with the mouth being either shut or open. Some practice it while suspending the breath and some do not.

Morsel 7

This if how to perform the meditation of three supports (*zikr-i se-paya*). Its form is imagined to be like an old-fashioned Grecian ewer that is a ceramic bowl which stands on three legs (*ibriq*). Like this ewer, this meditation rests on three things, and if one of them is missing the whole thing cannot stand firmly. This meditation depends on three conditions: first the

21. Literally this is known as the "babbling or chattering" meditation named after the sound that a stork makes (*laqlaqa* or "to babble" comes from *laqlaq* which signifies a stork), which is a continuous clucking or choking sound.

essential divine name Allah (*ism-i zat*), and second the three generative attributes of God (*sifat-i ummahat*) which are the One who knows (*'alim*), the One who hears (*sami'*), and the One who sees (*basir*), and thirdly the medium (*barzakh*). This meditation has seven conditions as stated in the poetic couplet:

> Medium, essence, attributes, drawing out, intensifying,
> below and above
> Show the spiritual seekers in each and every breath
> a taste of love
>
> *Barzakh o zat o sifat o madd o shadd o taht o fauq*
> *Mi-numayad taliban ra kulli nafas zauq o shauq*

Note carefully that the couplet is the same as that given in connection with the "meditation of negation and affirmation" (*zikr-i nafy o isbat*), but the explanation given in relation to his meditation differs significantly. In this meditation, "medium" (*barzakh*) refers to the form or face of one's spiritual guide, just as before. "Essence" (*zat*) refers to the essential name of God, namely Allah. In this meditation, "attributes" (*sifat*) refers to the three generative attributes of God which are the One who knows (*'alim*), the One who hears (*sami'*), and the One who sees (*basir*). "Intensifying" (*shadd*) refers to pronouncing the "l" with forceful heavy intensity. "Drawing out" (*madd*) refers to lengthening the initial "a" when pronouncing Allah. "Below" (*taht*) refers to starting to pronounce Allah from below the navel with force. "Above" (*fauq*) means that the pronunciation ends by being drawn upward towards the head (*dimagh*).[22]

This meditation of the three supports must always be practiced with suspending the breath (*habs-i nafas*), so this is not

22. The word *dimagh* means both mind and head. Here it signifies the head, or more specifically, the inner cavity of the head as the upper limit of the flow of breath.

specified in the above conditions. The mode of practicing it is this. The "a" of Allah is drawn with force from below the navel and the full breath is drawn up into the chest and there the breath is held compressed. Then one pronounces Allah with the heart coupled with *sami'*, while imagining its meaning "God hears." Then one pronounces Allah coupled with *basir*, while imaging its meaning "God sees." Then one pronounces Allah coupled with *'alim,* while imagining its meaning "God knows." Reciting this much with the in-breath is called "the ascent." Then one pronounces Allah coupled with each of these attributes in the inverse order: *'alim* for "God knows," *basir* for "God sees" and *sami'* for "God hears." This is called "the descent." Then one begins again to pronounce Allah with *sami'*, *basir* and *'alim* as at the start. This is called "the re-ascent."

The secret of the zikr lies in the fact that the sphere of hearing is less than that of seeing, and the sphere of seeing is less than that of knowing. The seeker begins in a state of reasoning about what is sensed (*'aql o shahadat*), the narrowest of all spiritual states. As the seeker moves beyond the attribute *sami'* or "hears," he progresses spiritually to a more comprehensive state of understanding what is beyond sensation (*ghayb*). As the seeker moves beyond the attribute *basir* or "sees," he progresses spiritually to a more comprehensive state of understanding beyond the beyond (*ghayb al-ghayb*). As the seeker moves through the attribute *'alim* or "knows," he comprehends this most expansive spiritual state. Then the seeker comes back through these attributes in the inverse order.

One should understand that a single cycle of this meditation consists of moving through these three attributes three times, like this: *Allah sami'*, *Allah basir*, *Allah 'alim* is the first ascent, then in inverse order *Allah 'alim*, *Allah basir*, *Allah sami'* is the descent, and then *Allah sami'*, *Allah basir*, *Allah 'alim* is the re-ascent. This process makes up one cycle of the meditation, with an ascent, then descent, then re-ascent. While reciting this with the heart, the breath must be suspended to such an extent that one repeats the above course two or three times with each breath. With practice, this can be extended to even more courses in each breath, up to 250 times! Doing this generates internal heat that will burn away the greasy fat that congeals around the heart and allows the whispering tempter (*khannas*) to cling to it.[23] When the heart is cleansed of this, tempting thoughts melt away and one is overpowered by blissful oblivion.

One should understand that starting to pronounce Allah from below the navel with force (*taht*) gives great advantages but presents many difficulties. Yet without it, this meditation of the three supports is rendered useless, so it should therefore be done as intensely as possible without straining oneself to the point of causing harm. May God keep you safe and secure!

To perform this meditation, one should sit cross-legged. With the big toe of the right foot and its neighboring toe, compress the sciatic nerve behind the left knee. Then draw in the abdomen around the navel towards the back, from below until above. Then close the eyes and call to the imagination the image of one's spiritual guide (*barzakh*). Then one begins by drawing the name Allah up from below the navel (*taht*) with great intensity while drawing out the initial "a" (*madd*) and emphasizing "la" (*shadd*). Then with the heart one observes the attributes "God hears" (*Allah sami'*), then "God sees" (*Allah basir*), then "God knows" (*Allah 'alim*). In some Sufi masters' books, this process is called "the descent," but this humble writer prefers to describe it as "the ascent," which should be followed by "the descent" and "re-ascent" as described above in detail.

With practice, this meditation can be mastered. Then, a single breath suspended can be extended so that the cycle of the meditation can be repeated 250 times. At this point,

---

23. The word given here for "greasy fat" is the Hindi term *dusumat*, whereas earlier he used the Persian term *charbi*.

one can add five more divine attributes: "God is from forever" (*Allah da᾿im*), "God is until forever" (*Allah qa᾿im*), "God is present" (*Allah hazir*), "God is watcher" (*Allah nazir*), and "God is witness" (*Allah shahid*). When, with practice, these extra attributes can be repeated 250 times with each suspension of breath such that the meditation is illumined by their light, then one can add seven more attributes. These attributes are called the "primary seven" divine attributes: "God lives" (*Allah hayy*), "God knows" (*Allah ʿalim*), "God does" (*Allah qadir*), "God desires" (*Allah murid*), "God hears" (*Allah samiʿ*), "God sees" (*Allah basir*) and "God speaks" (*Allah kalim*). When these are also mastered, one can expand the meditation to include divine attributes made up of compound names, such as: "God is most noble" (*Allah akram al-akrimin*), "God is most compassionate" (*Allah arham al-rahimin*), "God is most generous" (*Allah ajwad al-ajwadin*), "God is giver of great bounty" (*Allah zu᾿l-fadli᾿l-ʿazim*), and "God is lord of the great throne" (*Allah rabbu᾿ l-ʿarshi᾿l-ʿazim*).

Morsel 8

According to the Shattari Sufi order, "meditation of the three supports" can be performed while pronouncing the name of God, Allah, with the tongue or the heart, while the attributes—the names *samiʿ*, *basir* and *ʿalim* —are simply imagined in the mind. Always, the face or form of one's spiritual guide should be held in the imagination. The name Allah is begun from below the navel by drawing out the "a" (*madd*) and emphasizing the "la" (*shadd*). If the recitation reaches the top in one breath or stroke, they call this "the lesser war" (*muharaba saghira*). If the breath is suspended such that the name Allah with the divine attributes is repeated a hundred times during a single breath, they call this "the great war" (*muharaba kabira*). When the basic three divine attributes are mastered, then other attributes may be added while carefully preserving the pattern of ascent and descent. When performing this meditation as "the great war" one should suspend the breath with tremendous force and allow the meditation to be done through the medium of one's spiritual guide, with the result that the self is completely forgotten (*be-khudi*) and one is absent from one's senses (*be-hoshi*). This is better achieved after extensive fasting and long sleeplessness, and in this way the goal is attained in a shorter period.

Morsel 9

This is the method of performing "meditation on the name Allah in six beats" (*zikr-i shesh zarbi*) and its variation called "meditation on the name Allah in four beats" (*zikr-i chahar zarbi*). The "meditation of six beats" consists of repeating the divine name Allah towards each of the six directions (to the right, to the left, to the front, to the back, to above, and to below). A variation in four beats consists of sitting facing the direction to Mecca (*qibla*) and positioning in front of oneself the Qur'an or the tomb of a holy person, then reciting the name Allah towards the left, then towards the right, then towards in front towards the Qur'an or tomb, and lastly inwards towards the heart. When one does this repeatedly and gets engrossed in the meditation, one discovers unknown meanings of the Qur'an or secrets of the state of the holy person in the tomb. While doing this, hold the face or form of one's spiritual guide in the imagination as a medium, otherwise the meditation is futile.

Morsel 10

The "meditation of the blacksmith" (*zikr-i haddadi*) is performed by reciting "no god but God." One sits on one's knees with legs folded beneath. Then one faces to the left while beginning to pronounce "no God" (*la ilaha*) while drawing out the "la" (*madd*). Then as one pronounces this phrase, one rises up on one's knees to a great height and immediately repeats "but God" (*illa 'llah*) as a forceful blow down onto the heart while throwing oneself down into a seated position. One does this with the vehement force of a blacksmith striking hot iron with a heavy sledgehammer swung with both hands. Do this continuously until a spiritual sensation (*zauq*) is engendered. This method of meditation was taught by Imam Abu Hafs al-Haddad and it entails a lot of pain and effort.[24]

Morsel 11

This is the method of meditation by "observing the breath" (*pas-i anfas*). During the exhaled breath, one recites "no god" (*la ilaha*) and during the inhaled breath, one recites "but God" (*illa ʾllah*). One does this with each breath exhaled and inhaled while keeping one's concentration upon the navel as it is drawn in and extended out during breathing. After one does this meditation continuously and extensively, the meditation continues with one's breathing even if one is asleep or awake. If one achieves this level of continuous meditation in each breath, then the length of one's life is doubled.

Morsel 12

This meditation of "observing the breath" is sometimes taught such that one only recites the name Allah. The method of doing this is to recite the name Allah while extending the final letter "h" with a long "u" so that it takes on the sound of "*hu*."[25] While inhaling, one recites *Alla-* and when exhaling, one recites *-hu*. Doing this does not employ the voice; rather one lets the breath expresses the language of the heart. Other than this, the meditation is exactly like "observing the breath" as

24. Abu Hafs al-Haddad was a blacksmith who became a Sufi master of Nishapur in northern Persia, and he died in 787–89 CE. See Ahmet Karamustafa, *Sufism: the Formative Period* (Berkeley: University of California Press, 2007), 48.

25. In Arabic grammar, this is called pronouncing with *ashbaʿ* which extends the final vowel sound which is not an inherent part of the word and pronouncing it audibly. Saying God's name as *Alla-hu* gives it the implied meaning of "God is."

described above regardless of whether one recites the whole phrase *la ilaha illa 'llah*, or one recites only the name *Allahu*.

It may be that a sound is generated in the nose while performing this meditation. That sound is known as "nasal sawing" (*arra-i bini*). The friction and vibration of this sound creates zeal and passion, but it can make the head hot and dry. Almond oil can be applied to the nostrils and forehead to avoid this and perfect this meditation with no hinderance. Perfection is attained when the breath of the seeker does this meditation without his knowing or choosing it.

Sometimes a seeker is a bit simpleminded and inexperienced, and has trouble learning. Perhaps his heart is not yet inscribed with the voice of meditations and contemplations. In this case, its method can be imparted in the following way. The beginner sits respectfully on both knees, facing his spiritual guide who sits facing him knee to knee. The beginner is told to lower his chin onto his chest, draw his abdomen inward to the stomach and hold his chest out full. The beginner should close his eyes. Then his spiritual guide should begin to feel how the beginner breathes. As the beginner exhales fully, the guide should inhale for him, grafting his breath into the beginner's inhalation and exhalation. While thus engaged and joined together, the breath of the seeker will spontaneously cry out the recitation of "no god but God" (*la ilaha illa 'llah*) or *Allahu*, depending on which one is willed by the spiritual guide. This is no doubt amazing to observers! This cry of recitation might be so forceful that blood oozes from the beginner's nose and ears. In this way, the method of meditation can be transmitted from "bosom to bosom" and taught without the medium of words.

However, if one being taught is engaged in devotional exercises—especially contemplation that is done with suspending the breath—then the spiritual teacher can convey nothing to him in this way. This is because the one being taught is himself controlling his own breath. If the spiritual guide tries to graft his breath into the learner's breath while he is engaged in such contemplation, it could happen that the learner's unself-consciousness could overwhelm the spiritual guide such that it cancels out even the guide's thought to convey anything to the learner! This happened to the author in a Sufi gathering, with the result that the assembly was completely disrupted.

Morsel 13

This is the method of performing the "meditation for discovering the spirit" (*zikr-i kashf-i ruh*) through which one can discover the state of any spirit in any place. First, "Oh Lord" (*ya rabb*) is recited twenty-one times, then "Oh spirit of the spirit" (*ya ruh al-ruh*) is pronounced once with force upon the heart. Then raising the head, one recites "Oh spirit, just as God wills" (*ya ruh ma sha' Allah*). When this meditation is done, one fixes one's mind on the person whose state one desires to discover. Then the spirit of that person will appear to the seeker either in the waking state or in dream. If done 2,000 times, the subject will be speedily obtained. Khwaja Nasir al-Din Chiragh-i Delhi taught this method to Hazrat Sayyid Gisu Daraz.[26]

Morsel 14

Some spiritual guides teach that the compressed form of the entire blessed phrase "no god but God" (*la ilaha illa 'llah*) is to pronounce *Ha Hu Hi*. First *Ha* is recited to the right side, then *Hu* to the left, and then *Hi* towards the heart.

Morsel 15

This is a method of "meditation to discover the state of those in graves" (*zikr-i kashf-i qubur*). Sit close by the tomb or grave.

26. Shaykh Nasir al-Din Chiragh-i Delhi, "The Lamp of Delhi," was the chief disciple and successor to Shaykh Nizam al-Din Awliya in the Chishti Sufi order. He died in 1356. One of his chief disciples was Gisu Daraz ,"He with Long Locks," whose proper name was Sayyid Muhammad al-Husayni. He died in 1422 and is often seen as the patron saint of the Deccan region of South India, where he settled after leaving Delhi. See Syed Shah Khusro Hussaini, *Sayyid Muhammad al-Husayni-i Gisudiraz on Sufism* (Delhi: Idarah-i Adabiyat-i Delli, 1983).

Lift the head high and face towards the sky and say, "Reveal to me, oh light!" (*akshif li ya nur*). Then in a strong beat towards the heart say, "Reveal to me..." (*akshif li...*) and then with a beat towards the tomb of the deceased person say, "...what is his condition!" (... *ʿan halihi*). The state of the buried will be known in dream or otherwise.

Morsel 16

This is the method of "meditation for one's prayers to be answered" (*zikr li-ijaba al-daʿwat*). Make each beat through the medium of imagining one's spiritual guide (*rabita*). First say "Oh lord!" (*ya rabb*) to the right, then to the left, and lastly to the heart. Then in the same three beats and directions, say "Oh my lord!" (*ya rabbi*). One should repeat this meditation many times. When one desires to end the recitation, one lifts one's open hands up and passes them over the face repeating, "Oh my lord!" (*ya rabbi*). All this time, one should recall in the heart what is desired in one's prayers. The method of this meditation is given by the great master Ibn ʿArabi.[27]

Morsel 17

The basic principle meditation as taught in the Naqshbandi Sufi order is for the tip of the tongue to touch the palate and for the meditation to be done by suspending the breath. One begins by imagining "no" (*la*), taking this syllable from the navel and taken up to the head. Then one imagines "god" (*ilaha*) while inclining towards the right shoulder. Then one imagines "but God" (*illa ʾllah*) to the left side towards the heart with such force that the effect of it is felt in the whole body. The motion of this meditation is shown below in a diagram. The

27. Ibn ʿArabi was a Sufi master who unified mysticism with philosophy in a highly influential way. He was born in Andalusia, lived in North Africa and died in Damascus in 1240 CE; see Stephen Hirtenstein, *The Unlimited Mercifier: The Spiritual Life and Thought of Ibn ʿArabi* (Oxford: Anqa Publishing, 1999).

path of the motion corresponds to shape of the word "no" (*la*) when written in Arabic script.

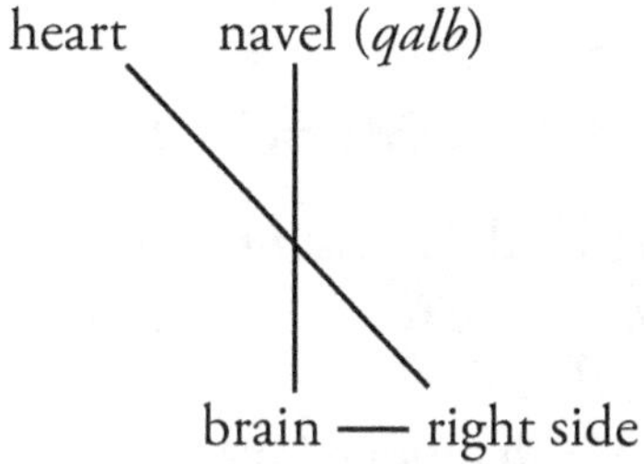

This form of meditation thus negates the false self and establishes the true One (*haqq*). One must say in the heart, "Oh God, you are my goal and I desire your contentment" (*Ilahi anta maqsudi wa rida'uka matlubi*). In his external form, the person performing this meditation must not show any outward motion at all while imagining these words of negation and affirmation (*la ilaha illa 'llah*). The number of times in which this phrase is repeated during one suspended breath must be an odd number—not an even number. When one exhales, one says in the heart, "Muhammad is the messenger of God" (*Muhammadun rasulu 'llahi*). The effect of performing this meditation is that by imagining the words of negation, one's self is negated and by imagining the words of affirmation, one's self is affirmed. If one repeats this meditation more than twenty-one times, yet still no effect is felt—no absence from the self or oblivion—one should stop and start over afresh, since some necessary condition of its proper method must have been neglected. Otherwise this type of meditation is effective enough to bring about its own result.

Morsel 18

This is the method of "meditation of affirmation and negation" (*zikr-i nafy o isbat*) in two beats or four beats. One recites "no god but God" (*la ilaha illa 'llah*) first towards the right side while imagining the Prophet Muhammad (peace and blessings be upon him), then towards the left side imagining one's own spiritual guide, then towards the heart, imagining God therein, and then facing a little further in towards one's center imagining absolute being.

Morsel 19

This is a method called "meditation for preventing illness" (*zikr-i daf-i marz*). Recite "Oh singular One!" (*ya ahad*) towards the right, then "Oh eternal One!" (*ya samad*) towards the left, and then "Oh unique One" (*ya witr*) towards the heart.

Morsel 20

This is a method called "meditation of the bountiful One" (*zikr-i wahhab*). After the canonical evening prayers, one must say supererogatory prayers of two cycles (*raka'at*). During each cycle, after one recites Surat al-Fatiha, then one recites Surat al-Ikhlas eleven times and says "Oh bountiful One!" (*ya wahhab*) seventy times. This method of meditation removes worldly needs and anxieties.

Morsel 21

This is called "meditation while walking step by step" (*zikr-i mashy-i aqdam*). If one is walking swiftly, one says "but God" (*illa 'llah*) at each step. If one is walking slowly, one says "no" (*la*) with the right step and "god" (*ilaha*) with the left step, and then "but" (*illa*) with the next right step and "God" (Allah) with the next left step. If one is walking at a medium pace, one simply says "God" (Allah) at every step.

Morsel 22

If one meditates with the entire phrase, saying "no god but God" (*la ilaha illa 'llah*) then this is known as meditation of the human realm (*nasut*). If one meditates with only the phrase "but God" (*illa 'llah*) this is known as meditation of the spiritual realm (*malakut*). If one meditates with only the name "God" (Allah) this is known as meditation of the archetypal realm (*jabarut*). And if one meditates with merely the pronoun "he" (*hu*) this is known as meditation of the divine realm (*lahut*).

Morsel 23

There are some meditation practices that spiritual masters transmit orally (from heart to heart) to disciples only after extensive training. This means only after disciples have undergone strenuous spiritual exercises (*riyazat*) and struggles (*mujahadat*) and have endured forty day retreats in order to purify the heart to the utmost.

From among these meditations is "the meditation of withness" (*zikr-i maʿiya*) in which one says, "Oh with me, oh with me, oh with me, oh he, oh he, oh he" (*ya maʿi, ya maʿi, ya maʿi, ya hu, ya hu, ya hu*). Performing this meditation enables one to witness the divine essence and attributes in a short period. The method of performing it is this. One sits as if in prayer (on one's knees), except that the feet should protrude out from under the shins, which should be resting on the ground. With the right hand, one should firmly hold the left arm, and with the left hand, one should hold firmly the right arm. Then one pronounces the following words in five beats. The first beat is directed to a spot between the knee and the right foot. The second beat is directed towards the sky. The third beat is directed towards the spot between the knee and the left foot. The fourth beat is directed towards one's liver. The fifth beat is directed towards one's heart with great intensity and force. One must keep in mind that *hu* is an expression for absolute unity that is like unto nothing else.[28] In the days when one is performing this meditation, one should drink milk especially if it is mixed with saffron. And one should use a lot of incense or fragrance. Sometime this meditation is abridged into the three

28. Surat al-Shura 42:11.

words, "He, he, oh with me" (*hu, hu, ya ma'i*). This is practiced as detailed above with the exception that *hu, hu* is pronounced towards the sky, and *ya ma'i* is pronounced towards the heart.

Another of these meditations is "the meditation of allness" (*zikr-i kulliya*). It consists of saying "All is with you, all is from you, all is to you, oh all of all!" (*bika 'l-kull, minka 'l-kull, ilayka 'l-kull, ya kulla 'l-kull*). But this humble writer has seen it in another form, saying "Oh God, you are all, and from you is all, and with you is all, and for you is all, and to you is all, oh all of all" (*Allahumma anta' l-kull wa minka' l-kull wa bika' l-kull wa laka' l-kull wa ilayka' l-kull wa kulla' l-kull*). Performing this enables one to behold the divine essence and attributes. To perform it, one sits cross-legged then makes one beat to the front, one beat to the right, one beat to the left side, one beat to the sky, and one beat to the heart.

Another of these is "the meditation of all-encompassing" (*zikr-i ihata*). It consists of saying, "Oh you who encompass all without and all within" (*ya muhit zahran wa batnan*). One opens one's eyes when saying "all without" and one closes one's eyes when saying "all within." It bestows the experience of witnessing the divine (*mushahada*).

Another of these is "the meditation of obliterating all directions" (*zikr-i mahw al-jihat*). In this practice, one says "You are above me, you are beneath me, you are before me, you are behind me, you are right of me, you are left of me, you are in me, and I am with you in all directions—wherever you may turn there is the face of God!" (*Anta fauqi, anta tahti, anta amami, anta khalfi, anta yamini, anta shamali, anta fiya wa ana ma' al-jihati fika—aynama tawallu fa-thumma wajhu' llahi*).[29] It is performed in this way. One stands and faces the heavenly throne to say "You are above me" (*anta fauqi*). Then one turns to face the earth and sits to say, "You are below me" (*anta tahti*). Then sitting one turns to face towards the front to say,

29. This phrase quotes Qur'an 2:115: "To God is the east and the west. Wherever you may turn there is the face of God."

"You are before me" (*anta amami*). Then still sitting, one turns one's head to the rear to say, "You are behind me" (*anta khalfi*). Turning to face the right one says, "You are right of me" (*anta yamini*). Turning to face to the left one says, "You are left of me" (*anta shamali*). Then in a beat directed to the heart one says, "You are in me" (*anta fiya*). After this one says, "and I am with you in all directions—wherever you may turn there is the face of God!" (*wa ana ma' al-jihati fika ... aynama tawallu fa-thumma wajhu' llahi*).[30]

Another of these is "the meditation of manifesting self-hood" (*zikr-i tajalli-yi ana' iya*). It consists of saying, "I am God, there is no god but I" (*inni ana allah la ilaha illa ana*). After late-night vigil prayers (*tahajjud*) this phrase should be pronounced 100 times in the following manner. Lifting the head towards heaven, one recites "I am God" (*inni ana allah*). Then one lowers the head towards the right side and says "there is no god..." (*la ilaha*) and then pronounces towards the heart with great force "... but I" (*illa ana*). In all above five meditations, it is required that one holds in the imagination the meaning of the words and also the image of one's spiritual guide (*barzakh*).

Another of these is a meditation done by Hazrat Shaykh Shakar Ganj.[31] This meditation is in the Punjabi language. One says, "Above is you" (*uhul tun*) indicating the celestial worlds. One says, "Below is you" (*ihul tun*) indicating the terrestrial worlds. One says, "You are only you" (*tuhin tun*) indicating the ultimate absolute.

Morsel 24

When an assembly for meditation is finished, one should repeat three times: "Glory be to God, may God be praised. Glory

30. This final phrase is taken from Surat al-Baqara 2:115.

31. This refers to Shaykh Farid al-Din Mas'ud who was nick-named Ganj-i Shakar or "Treasury of Sugar." He was the spiritual guide of Shaykh Nizam al-Din Awliya in the Chishti Sufi Order. Shaykh Farid al-Din lived in Punjab and died at Ajodhan (known as Pakpattan, in Pakistan) in 1265 CE; see K. A. Nizam, *The Life and Times of Shaikh Farid-u'd-Din Ganj-i-Shakar* (Delhi: Idarah-i Adabiyat-i Delli, 1955).

to be God most great and may he be praised" (*subhan 'llahi wa bi-hamdi-hi subhana 'llahi 'l-'azim wa bi-hamdi-hi*).

Further this prayer should be said: "Oh God, you said 'So remember me that I remember you' and I have remembered you to the meager degree of my knowledge, reason and understanding. Remember me with the bounteous capacity of your self, your blessing, your knowledge and your forgiveness. Oh God, open the ears of our hearts with your remembrance, oh you, who are the best of those who remember."[32]

Chapter 2: On Methods of Contemplation

You should know that contemplation (*muraqaba*) is a way for one to protect one's heart such that it cleaves to one single meaning and no other. There are three things that cause the heart to fall ill so that is gets distracted from the true One (*haqq*). First, there is the speech of the self (*hadith-i nafs*) which is constantly bombarding the heart with motives and willful choices, either overtly or covertly. Secondly, there are tempting thoughts (*khatra*) which come and go without one's own motivation. Thirdly, there is observing phenomena that are other than God in this world of multiplicity. To cure the illness of the heart one must do internal work (*shughl-i batin*). This is contemplation, and it is of various types.

Morsel 1

One can contemplate the greatest divine name, the name of the essence, namely Allah. One must displace the speech of the self and put Allah in its place. One can contemplate the primal qualities of the divine (*sifat-i ummahat*).[33] One must displace

32. In Arabic this prayer read: *"Allahumma innaka qulta fa-zkuruni azkurakum wa qad zakartuka 'ala qadri qillati 'ilmi wa 'aqli wa fahmi. fa-zkurni 'ala qadri sa'ati nafsika wa fadlika wa 'ilmika wa maghfiratika. Allahummma iftah masami'a qulubina bi-zikrika, ya khaira 'l-zakirin."*

33. The primal attributes of the divine are life (*hayat*), knowledge (*'ilm*), power (*qudra*), will (*irada*), hearing (*sam'*), sight (*basar*), and speech (*kalam*), as mentioned above in Chapter 1, Morsel 2.

tempting thoughts and put the primal qualities of the divine in their place. One must keep the gaze of the heart directed upon the beauty of one's spiritual guide which is called the medium (*wasita*) or connection (*rabita*) or betweenness (*barzakh*).

Morsel 2

One should observe Allah as the holy and wholly other essence (*ma'na muqaddas*) that is beyond any limits or specifications that are commonly understood. One should meditate on that essence with the entire concentration of the organ of one's heart (*dil-i sanubari*), until the eternity and splendor of this essence causes one's intellect to be brightened and one's constitution to be purified. If one's mind cannot comprehend the holy and wholly other essence, then one can imagine it as a pure and undifferentiated light. One may imagine that one is dissolved in the light, as if it were an ocean of light and one were a mere drop within it. Or one can conceive of the holy and wholly other essence as utter and impenetrable darkness. One can imagine that one is dissolved into that darkness, as if one were a mere shadow, for when a shadow merges with darkness it vanishes, and all differentiation ceases.

Morsel 3

Some sages explain that when one practices contemplation one must hold the image of one's spiritual guide in the imagination, so that the one exercising might feel his heat and spiritual presence. In this way, one can focus upon one's own human, all-comprehensive spiritual reality in the form of one's spiritual guide. In other words, one grasps one's own essential humanity by holding fast the image of one's spiritual guide. One imagines the essence of humanity to be concentrated in one's own spiritual guide. One's all-comprehensive spiritual reality is, in the technical vocabulary of Sufis, called the heart (*qalb*). Because this spiritual reality is transcendent and cannot be limited to incarnation in bodies, realizing it is not easy. In order to mitigate this difficulty, one can concentrate upon the flesh of the heart in which dwells the essential heart. This fleshy organ is the metaphorical heart that has a relation to the essential heart, a relation enjoyed by no other part of the body. One should focus one's full concentration upon the heart, such that all one's sensory awareness becomes unified in one direction and upon one object. There can be no doubt that when this state is achieved, self-absence and unselfconsciousness will manifest. One can imagine that this state of absence is a clear path that is smooth and straight. One can then imagine that one is traveling along this path which is an endless path. Whenever any selfish thought (*khatra*) or temptation (*waswas*) distracts one, one begins to slip and slide off the path. Such thoughts can either be shaken off or they take possession of one. If shaken off, that is the intended goal. If they are not shaken off and they begin to take possession of one, then one must concentrate on that spiritual reality that is apprehended as the image of one's spiritual guide, and by this means one can ward them off. In this way, one can find help from the presence of one's spiritual guide. But if these distractions are not warded off, then one must clear one's mind by exhaling the breath through the nostrils with great force. Then one settles back into concentrating as one did before.

If this is not effective, the following prayer for forgiveness must be recited over and over with both tongue and heart in union: "I seek forgiveness of God. I seek forgiveness of God from all that is repulsive to God in word and deed, in open and in secret, in what is heard and what is seen. There is no power and no strength save in God, the lofty One, the great One."[34]

---

34. In Arabic this prayer reads: *"Astaghfiru ʾllaha min jamiʿi ma kariha ʾllahu qawlan wa fiʿlan wa hadiran wa ghaʾiban wa samiʿan wa naziran, wa la hawla wa la quwwata illa bi-llahi ʾl-ʿaliyi ʾl-ʿazimi."*

If still the distractions are not warded off, then one may imagine the name of God, "Oh effective One!" (*ya fa'al*) because it has a special quality of removing distracting temptations. If this provides no benefit, then one can consider the phrase "no god but God" (*la ilaha illa 'llah*) as meaning "no existence but God" (*la mawjuda illa 'llah*). If this is found to be of no benefit, then one must recite with the name Allah with intensification (*shadd*) and elongation (*madd*) and direct it with a forceful beat onto the heart.

Morsel 4

Whatever is perceived by the senses both external and internal is not devoid of meaning. Rather, if what is sensed is in accord with reality (*waqi'a*) then it is truth (*haqq*). And if what is sensed does not accord with reality then it is non-truth *(batil)*. Those who believe in the "Oneness of Being" (*wahdat-i wujud*) hold that God manifests in the appearance of truth, but also manifests in the appearance of non-truth. Shaykh Abu Madyan Maghribi, who was the spiritual guide of Shaykh Ibn 'Arabi, expresses this idea in the following quatrain.[35]

Do not always deny what is not true
for sometimes God appears there too
Obey God in whatever way you can
So you affirm God's reality as is due

la tunkir al-batilla fi tawri-hi
fa-inna-hu ba'da zahurati-hi
wa a'ti-hu min-ka bi-miqdari-hi
hata tawafiya haqqa ithbati-hi

35. Abu Madyan Shu'ayb ibn al-Hussain al-Ansari was born near Seville and died in Tlemcen, Algeria, in 1198. He is considered to be a pioneer Sufi shaykh of Western Islamic lands (*maghrib,* meaning Andalusia and North Africa). For his life, teachings and poems, see Vincent Cornell, *The Way of Abu Madyan* (Cambridge: Islamic Texts Society, 1996).

To complete this idea, Shaykh Mu'ayyid al-Din al-Jandi added a rhyming couplet.[36]

> Divinity can appear in human form, too
> so don't deny your essence as the foolish do
>
> *fa 'l-haqqu qad yazharu fi surati-hi*
> *wa yunkiru al-jahil fi dhati-hi*

So therefore, whatever one senses of universal principles (*kulliyat*) or sensory things (*juz'iyat*) should be understood as witnessing the absolute being which manifests in a particular form at that moment. Contemplating this is the best spiritual path and the most reliable way to stop the incoming stream of selfish thoughts. Beyond a doubt, it causes a state of self-absence and provides an experience of bliss. It allows one to comprehend the differentiated levels (*maratib*) of divinity and materiality. But it is best that you negate all such phenomenal appearances while affirming the spiritual experience of self-absence, so that you pass away from your egoistic self (*nafs-i khud*) and embrace unselfconsciousness. In the view of the sages of this Sufi path, it is infidelity to cling to whatever comes to you in a state of self-absence (*ghaybat*). However, what comes to you in this state may have connected with it concentration, insight into profound spiritual realities and subtle realizations of knowledge and experience. The benefit provided to you by states of self-absence and unselfconsciousness can be the

36. To explain this point further, the editor of Shaykh Kalimullah's text writes: "It is said that God sometimes appears in the form of a human being, but foolish and ignorant this. This is proved by the verse of Qur'an that says, 'God makes the truth true and people denounce makes un-truth false even if those who denounce detest it'" (Surat al-Anfal 8:8). Shaykh Mu'ayyid al-Din al-Jandi was a Sufi in Ibn Arabi's school of thought, which some authors call "theosophical Sufism." He was a disciple of Sadr al-Din Qunawi, the step-son of Ibn Arabi and his most authoritative interpreter. Al-Jandi wrote a commentary on Ibn Arabi's famous text, *Fusus al-Hikam;* see William Chittick and Peter Lamborn Wilson (trans. and ed.), *Fakhruddin 'Iraqi—Divine Flashes* (Mahwah, NJ: Paulist Press, 1982), xvi, 44 and 65.

beginning of bewilderment (*hayrat),* which is the final stage of the spiritual path.

Morsel 5

The spiritual seeker should look within with the eye of the heart to perceive his or her own truth which is an expression for all-comprehensive spiritual reality of the self (*haqiqa-yi jamiʿiya-yi u*). In this way, the seeker keeps the essential reality of his self under observation with the heart's eye in all actions and all states. The seeker sees that all things that exist in the world—be they good or bad, subtle or gross, sensory or spiritual—are reflections of the all-comprehensive spiritual reality of the self, until the seeker perceives that the whole cosmos and all worlds are established and sustained through it. Then all things that are sensed or thought are mere reflections that are seen as effects of it (the all-comprehensive spiritual reality of the self). It is as if the entire cosmos were the body and the seeker's self were the soul animating that body. This station is known as "comprehending comprehensiveness" (*jamʿ al-jamʿ*). When this contemplation is powerfully mastered, the seeker will be aware of all things in the cosmos, and if they are joyful he will feel joy, and if they are sorrowful he will feel sorrow. This is because the soul feels the rewards and sufferings that result in the action of the body, regarding whether the body performs what is obligatory and desists from what is prohibited.

Morsel 6

Another method of contemplation is to look at the written form of "no god but God" (*la ilaha illa ʾllah*) or simply the name "God" (Allah). One can look at this form with the eye of the head as it is written on paper, or one can look at it with the gaze of insight as it is written on the paper of knowledge or the tablet of imagination. One should become so engrossed in contemplating this form until unselfconsciousness overcomes one, and one is oblivious to that form and unaware even of being oblivious to that form.

Morsel 7

Another method is to contemplate some object such as a stone, a clod, a grave, the Qur'an, a beloved person's face, one's spiritual guide's face, a flower or other such thing. One should gaze upon this object with one's physical eyes and not move one's eyelids to blink. One should also focus one's inner concentration, through that object, upon the absolute reality that is essential and unchanging. One should persist with this until selfish thoughts cease, and one is overwhelmed with unselfconsciousness and one is oblivious to all things, even to the fact that one is oblivious. This method of contemplation is attributed to the Sufi master Ibrahim ibn Adham Balkhi.[37]

Morsel 8

Some great masters of the Sufi path say that the following is the best way to contemplate God and enter into the presence of the divine, glorified be God and lofty be God's state! One should retire one's personal powers—both inward and outward, both universal and sensorial—from dispersive actions, and one should clear one's mind of all knowledge or belief, indeed, from anything that is other than God. Then one should concentrate on God simply as what God is, without limiting God by any mental conception of transcendence or immanence (*na bi tanzih ya bi tashbih*). One should concentrate with a universal concentration upon the most essential aspect of divinity which is received by every form, whether it be considered good and beautiful, or bad and awful, whether it be perceptible by

37. Ibrahim ibn Adham was an important early Sufi master who died in 777 AH in Syria. According to his legend, he was a ruler in Balkh (present-day Afghanistan) who abdicated his position in order to become an ascetic and mystic. The Chishti Sufi Order traces its lineage back through him to early Sufi masters and then to Imam Ali and the Prophet Muhammad.

the senses or beyond the senses. One should concentrate on this with belief in oneness (*tawhid*) and firm determination (*ʿazimat*) and force of will (*jamʿiyat*) and pure sincerity (*ikhlas*) in a constant and continuous way. One should concentrate in this way until one no longer experiences distraction in thought and dispersal in determination. One should realize that the utter perfection of God encompasses all possible qualities, whether someone might perceive them to be good or bad. One should realize that reason or thought or imagination cannot possibly fathom even the hidden secrets of divine nature. God is simply what God is. If God wills, the divine manifests in any form of the cosmos or in all forms of the cosmos. And if God wills, the divine transcends them and is beyond them all.

Morsel 9

The seeker may contemplate the self as being the origin of divine disclosures rather than being the consequence of divine disclosures (*tajalliyat*). The seeker should keep this view constantly in sight. In this way, one should see all things as both absolute being (*wujudi mutlaq*) and limited being (*wujudi muqayyad*), with reality being that both types are indeed one. For naming something as absolute or naming something as limited are relative to the perspective and judgment of the observer. If one persists with this contemplation for a long time, it will induce intense spiritual experience (*zauq*).

Morsel 10

Another method is to close the eyes and fix the gaze on the heart, then stay aware that God is present and watching and that God is with you.

Morsel 11

Another method is to keep one's eyes open and strive to not blink while staring upwards or directly ahead. This generates some light and heat issues from the eyelids to spread all through the body, generating a feeling of passionate love.

Morsel 12

Another method is known as "Station of Aid" (*maqam-i nasir*). One should keep one's eyes open and gaze on the tip of the nose with such intensity that the blackness of the eye (the pupil) disappears and only whiteness of the eyes appears. This produces a tranquil composure and wards off selfish thoughts. This is known as "Station of Aid." During the practice one may chose to sit as in prayer (on one's knees) or on all fours like a dog. If one does the practice as described above but fixes the gaze between the eyebrows, it is called the "Praised Station" (*maqam-i mahmud*). The benefits accruing from this meditation are many.[38]

Morsel 13

The Yogis have eighty-four positions (*bethak*) and each one has its own peculiar benefit. Shaykh Baha᾿ al-Din Qadiri selected one as a position that comprehends all the other positions and he described it like this.[39] One sits on the ground cross-legged, bringing the legs together so that the heel of the left foot rests

38. These two terms are discussed in greater detail in reference to the *Treatise on the Human Body* below.

39. This refers most likely to Shaykh Baha al-Din Ibrahim Shattari of Burhanpur, who was also member of the Qadiri Order, as he is named here. In Burhanpur and the Deccan, most Shattari Sufis also held allegiance to the Qadiri Sufi Order, and gradually the two became thoroughly fused. Shaykh Baha al-Din and other Shattari Sufis were very active in integrating Sufi meditation techniques with Yoga; in his only known writing, he explained, "Another way of meditation in the *Hindawi* language is to sit cross-legged, just as the Yogis do. Raise your eyes and face to the heavens. Pronounce the following words of meditation one thousand times or more, and it will let you achieve in the end the realm of spiritual flight"; from Baha᾿ al-Din Shattari Burhanpuri, *Risala Shattariyya* (manuscript at Hyderabad: Andhra Pradesh State Oriental Manuscript Library, 745 Farsi Tasawwuf), 46.

below one's testicles and the heel of the right foot is placed close to it. Then one rests one's seat down. Then one draws the breath upward pulling in the navel towards the back. One keeps the mouth closed and cleaves the tongue firmly to the palate. Then one stays busy in contemplation. Internally, one imagines the sounds "*U He He*." One continues this practice without eating or sleeping. If the practice is continued without a break for three days, refraining from eating and sleeping, it will result in a state of unselfconsciousness and oblivion in which hidden spiritual realities are revealed. One might then return to one's senses or one might become mad (*majzub*) or senseless (*madhosh*). If the desired effect does not happen after three days of this practice, it may be extended for another three days continuously. But between every three-day period, one should eat, drink and sleep for a while lest lunacy occurs. In this way, one may extend it extensively.

Morsel 14

This is another method of contemplation leading to witnessing (*mushahada*) and beholding (*mu'ayyana*). One should sit as in prayer, then observe the practice of "God is knowing" (*'alim*), "God is hearing" (*sami'*), and "God is seeing" (*basir*) while maintaining connection (*rabt*) with one's spiritual guide and all the proper conditions.[40] When one gets firmly established in this practice, then one can sit in this form and incline one's face towards the heart. Then one closes the eyes and, with the eyes of the heart, one gazes upon the heart and there one imagines that one is seeing God. When one gets firmly established in this practice, then one can sit as before, but one gazes towards the sky with one's eyes open and one imagines "My soul left the body and has passed beyond the heavens and is engrossed in beholding God (*mu'ayyana-i haqq ta'ala*). When

40. This reference is to the practice of "Meditation of the Three Supports" as described above in Chapter 1, Morsel 7.

one gets firmly established in this practice, one will see a green cord connecting on one end to above the seventh heaven and on the other end to within one's heart. This is the highest level of reflection (*fikr*). It is a practice that Sufi masters used to keep secret. In this practice, it is not correct to hold the image of one's spiritual guide as a medium (*wasita*) for this meditation.

The first stage of this practice is known as contemplation (*muraqaba*). The second stage is known as witnessing (*mushahada*). The third stage is known as beholding (*mu'ayyana*). Shaykh Nasir al-Din Chiragh-i Delhi attributed these practices to Shaykh Nizam al-Din.[41]

Morsel 15

Sayyid Muhammad Gisu Daraz says that one should be silent and think that "I am not, God is" (*man nay-am u-st*). This is expressed in a couplet of Persian poetry.

> I am not, by God oh my friends, I am not
> I am soul's life, heart's secret, body I am not
>
> *man nay-am, wa'llah yaran, man nay-am*
> *jan-i jan-am, sirr-i sirr-am, tan nay-am*

When the meaning of this dawns to one's thoughts, then a voice calls out "You are I," in accord with the verse of Qur'an "Truth has come and untruth disappears."[42] This is the most effective and efficient method of spiritual realization.

---

41. The text reads "Sultan-Jiu Nizam al-Din" and here refers to Nizam al-Din Awliya by his honorific title, "Sultan-i Awliya" or Chief of the Saints. Nizam al-Din was the spiritual guide of Shaykh Nasir al-Din, who was in turn the spiritual guide of Muhammad Hussaini Gisu Daraz, referred to next.

42. Surat al-Isra 17:81.

Morsel 16

The whole cosmos becomes manifest (*tajalli*) to those who are engaged in contemplation and meditation on God. Bayazid Bistami, the chief of all sages (*Sultan al-ʿArifin*), was engaged in this from the cradle to the grave. [43]

Morsel 17

This is a method of contemplation called "Ascension of the Sages" (*miʿraj al-ʿarifin*). You imagine all existing things as a multitude of mirrors. Then all that you see in them of sensory and rational phenomena you should understand as reflections of the forms of the names and attributes of God. Then imagine them and indeed the entire cosmos as a single mirror, and gaze into it in order to see the face of God with all the divine names and attributes. Do this until you become one of the people who witness divine reality (*mushahada*) just as you started out as one of the people who receive divine inspiration (*mukashafa*). Then go further and observe that you see yourself like the whole cosmos, and know that your essence encompasses everything existing and that everything existing is formed within you. Come to realize that your essence is a mirror in which all things are reflected. Just as in the beginning you saw God reflected in all things other than yourself, now you witness God reflected within your self. Then go further and observe that all potential things are in themselves really nonexistent (*mumkinat min haythu hiya ghayr mawjuda*). So disregard them entirely, such that all things appear to you as forms of God's self-disclosure that exist only as God supports them. All things are merely divine beauty and perfection in which you are witnessing God. Then go further and disregard the being of your own self in order to

---

43. Bayazid Bistami was an early Sufi master from Iran who died in 874 CE, who championed the superiority of mystical intoxication over rational sobriety; see Schimmel, *Mystical Dimensions of Islam,* 47-51.

witness God alone and comprehend the divine essence, which is both the one witnessing and the one witnessed (*wa huwa 'l-shahid wa' l-mashhud*).

Morsel 18

The Naqshbandi Sufi order bases its devotional exercises on three different ways. The first way consists of spiritual concentration (*tawajjuh*) and contemplation on the divine essence as being without qualities and qualifications, without similarities and appearances, as is understood from the blessed divine name Allah, by which means it is expressed in languages like Arabic and Persian and others. In this way, Naqshbandi Sufis concentrate with all their force and focus until they become easily accustomed to perpetually apprehending it, and the way is opened to the spiritual experiences of "obliteration of obliteration" (*fana'-i fana'*).

The second way consists of contemplation through a medium (*rabita*). This is concentration upon the form of one's spiritual guide (*tawajjuh bi-surat-i shaykh*) who is obliterated in God and sustained with God. One does this until a state of self-absence and unselfconsciousness are manifest. Then the physical form of the medium (*barzakh*), which is the lowest aspect of the spiritual guide, disappears from one's sight, and one's sight is focused only on the wide ocean of witnessing the essence and presence of God which is the highest aspect of the spiritual guide.

The third way consists of silent meditation upon the phrase "no god but God" (*la ilaha illa 'llah*) which includes both negation and affirmation.

The first way of concentrating directly upon God is the most lofty and noble, but attaining it is difficult until the spiritual seeker is pulled by divine attraction (*jazba*) towards God. The second way of concentrating on the form of one's spiritual master is the shortest of all the paths, and through it comes experiences both wondrous and strange. The third way of meditation is most reliable and it is the foundation of all exercises.

Morsel 19

One should gaze for a long time in a mirror until, when you look at your own face, you imagine it to be the face of your spiritual guide and this perception becomes firm and fixed. Keep up this gazing until you attain a state of self-absence from your senses.

Morsel 20

One should gaze at the name of God (Allah) written in characters of silver or gold ink, fixing one's sight on it. Similarly, one could inscribe the name of God in one's imagination upon the scroll of the heart and then concentrate upon it until one attains a state of self-absence from the senses.

Conclusion

All that which is written in the two preceding chapters deserves your careful attention—and may God seal your good deeds with the best of seals. Anyone who takes up these varieties of meditation and types of contemplation will surely attain the goal (of God-consciousness). But anyone who tries them without firm resolve, persistent practice and total absorption will find the goal far away. To fancy that a mere perusal of these pages without practice will bring success will reveal one's vanity. It proves the saying that "this world depends on actions not words." The harder one practices the further one gets. The Sufi master Abu Hafs al-Haddad states, "Sufism is merely cooking what one imagines until it is done." The reality is that when certain imaginings become cooked and ripe and enter the mind of the soul, strange and wondrous effects are seen in both common people and spiritual masters, effects that produce a delight in those who experience them and provoke astonishment in those who look on.

But there are selfish people who call themselves Sufis yet are content with a mere knowledge of the variety of meditation and contemplation practices. In their case, we hope for the largess of God's patient restraint, which surely is vaster than their sins, and if not, then they surely will come to ruin. Some people like this descend even lower, and in order to earn a good reputation in the eyes of others they dabble in these practices for a short time; yet when they fail to feel any effect or spiritual delight, they give up in despair and become engrossed in worldly aspirations. And some others with scanty progress are filled with pride and proclaim themselves to be spiritual masters, and dupe people and fall into that whirlpool. But what does it benefit a sinful man to follow a sinful man? I take refuge with God from such people, and you should too!

A real spiritual master is one who takes to the spiritual path and yet, until he really feels its effect and can affect others, refrains from announcing himself to others and calling attention to himself. This modest caution is more than enough to warn the negligent, and under God's command are all affairs.

Now to the point, this conclusion describes the special way that a disciple of right understanding experiences meditation. Were he to begin with a righteous disposition and according to the instructions detailed, there is every hope that he would advance quickly and steadily from stage to stage and in the shortest time achieve a state of spiritual comprehensiveness (*jam*ʿ). Some of these experiences I have already alluded to in the midst of describing the various methods of meditation. But God is the ultimate dispenser of success, and any benefit that one gets should be looked for with God, upon whom I trust in every moment and every deed.

Morsel 1

You should know that everything that can be known is either essential (*basit*) or compound (*murakkab*). If one knows something to be singular, that is the same from every direction and in every condition, then it is necessarily knowledge and apprehension of an essential thing. If one knows something to be multiple, yet one knows it in a general way as singular, then this is also knowledge of an essential thing. Surely the first case is knowledge of a thing that is essential in its reality, and the second is knowledge of a thing that is essential in its effect. If something is known which is not singular from every direction and in every condition, or which is multiple yet is seen in general as single, then there is no doubt that it is a thing compound. The community of Sufis who strive for purity are those who endeavor to leave aside anything known as compound and cleave to that which is known as essential, namely to the one necessary being (*wajib al-wajud*, a philosophical term for God). They do this in such a way that at all times, or at least in most times, they are engrossed in comprehension of that singular essential being and ignore the distracting multiplicity of things other than this. In this way, being obliterated in God (*fana᾽ fi ᾽llah*) is obliterating everything other than God and ultimate obliteration is obliterating any sense of this obliteration!

Morsel 2

One should sit in an isolated corner, facing towards the direction of Mecca, with full ritual ablutions. One should close the eyes and cleave the tongue firmly to the palette. One should imagine that "the flesh of the heart is saying Allah, but I do not hear it" and one should strive to hear it. One should summon one's firmest resolve to hear it. After some time, with the aid of God's grace, one will begin to feel a vibration which may be understood to be the motion of the heart or the motion of the egoistic self (*nafs*) or the motion of tempting thoughts (*waswas*). When one reaches this point, one must summon even more firm resolve so that this vibration becomes more apparent, such that it overwhelms the motion of the egoistic self and of tempting thoughts. Then one knows by experience that the flesh of the heart is moving with a vibration that says Allah. When one has been blessed with this happiness, then one can summon the spiritual aspiration to listen—whether alone or in the company of others—for the silent speech of one's own heart. At this point, one realizes that the heart is perpetually meditating on God by repeating the name Allah. Realizing this spiritual fortune is the true goal of every devotional exercise, though some achieve it sooner and some later, some with slight effort and some with intense concentration. As the Qur᾿an says, "Never despair of being with God's spirit for indeed the only ones who despair of God's spirit are those who are unbelievers."[44]

Morsel 3

Sometimes it happens that the flow of breathing obscures one's ability to hear this vibration. To prevent this, the breath should be suspended just beneath the navel. In this way, the heart becomes like water, tranquil in a basin, that is preserved from being obscured by any waves or agitation and therefore can reflect the image of something other than itself. One should be careful not to suspend the breath to such an extent that one becomes deadly sick. Still, the danger of suspending the breath is less than the danger of never suspending it. Suspending the breath should be done according to one's own capacity. And when the suspending breath is exhaled, it should be released gradually and gently, and during exhaling also one should pay close attention to the heart's vibration.

Morsel 4

Once one becomes aware of this vibration and the heart is known to be continuously meditating (with God's name), then one must try to preserve this awareness. Initially, awareness of this will be so weak that in a mere moment or with the least distraction one can forget it. One cannot always be aware of it when one tries, yet one must continually try, because to stop trying is the cause of losing spiritual concentration such that awareness of this vibration is lost. One should never succumb to discontent or despair! Rather, one should keep trying, while

44. Surat Yusuf 12:87.

acknowledging one's inability and weakness and waywardness and humbleness. Most often, one loses hold of this vibration because of the incessant speaking of the ego (*hadith-i nafs*) or tempting thoughts or distracting knowledge of the multiplicity of existing things, as mentioned earlier at the start of the last chapter. It is impossible for the heart to attend to two things at one and the same time.

Morsel 5

When this great experience is finally realized, one should not think it a light and trifling thing. Rather, one should strive to cultivate one's connection to it day and night. If some other indispensable affair commands one's attention, one may put it aside for a while. If other kinds of worship, like supererogatory prayers or reciting litanies or reading Qur᾽an, interfere with one's connection to this vibration, then one should put them aside. But if these acts of worship do not interfere with it, then one should continue with them, for perhaps that will aid one to maintain one's connection with it.

Little by little, one may open one's eyes and still find that one maintains this connection and is still present with it. One should do this until one is able to keep one's eyes open yet still fix one's concentration upon the heart. This is called "alone in the midst of company" (*khilvat dar anjuman*). With divine aid, one finds that this connection with the heart grows in strength, such that if one gets distracted one can, with just the slightest concentration, find it again. When it is found again, this connection will last even longer and becomes extended. Soon, despite everything that interrupts and distracts one, this connection is maintained and does not dissipate. At this stage, one discovers the true delight of constant remembering (*iltizaz-i zikr*) and one attains spiritual comprehension (*jam῾iyat*).

Morsel 6

When the vibration reaches the point when one hears the voice of the heart reciting the name of God with no difficulty, then this vibration—which was formerly concentrated in the pine-cone shaped organ of the heart (*dil-i sanubari*)—begins to spread all over the body. The vibration spreads in such a way that it manifests in one part of the body. Just as one sensed this vibration emitting from the heart, one will begin to sense it emitting from that other part of the body. But one should not turns one's attention to that part of the body but rather continue to focus one's concentration upon the heart. One senses sometimes that the vibration is coming from the hand, or sometimes from the foot or the head, without one's willing this to take place. But one should not pay attention to vibration in the limbs lest it distract one from the heart. In this matter, the heart is source and master, and the limbs of the body merely follow it.

Morsel 7

When the light of remembrance begins to spread, it quickly expands to encompass regions of the body until it fills one from the top of the head to the lowest toenail. Then all the various spiritual states will manifest themselves, and sometimes one will feel happy and elated, at other times one will feel anxious and bewildered, and other times one will feel sorrow and crying. But one should not be distracted by these states and should stay engrossed in meditative remembrance as the most important duty in one's religion and worldly life.

With divine aid, one might reach the point when one hears the whole entire body resonate with the name of God (Allah*)*. Then all parts of the body resonate in harmony with the heart and call out with one voice and one tone. The vibration preponderates sometimes in some parts of the body more than in others, and sometimes it is felt equally in all of them. When it resonates equally in all of them, one experiences a more intense delight. In Sufi terms, this is known as "The Prime Recitation" (*sultan al-zikr*).

Morsel 8

At first, recitation of the heart happens without the help of actually hearing it. But gradually, when recitation gets firmly fixed in the heart, then one usually hears it more and more clearly with one's ears. To a seeker with a pure personality, the ability to hear the heart becomes stronger and stronger all by itself.

Some contend that when one can hear the reciting voice of the heart it can be overheard by others. Indeed, it is a popular misconception that if one can hear one's own heart vibrating with recitation that this can be heard by others as well. Some are of the opinion that the voice of the reciting heart can be heard by others from close or from afar, in accord with differing capacities of reciters and listeners, but this is a baseless claim. Shaykh Sharaf al-Din Yahya Maneri, the author of *Mine of Meanings* (*Maʿdin al-Maʿani*), indicates this. If some support this popular conception, it may be as one performs this meditative recitation in the chest, a feeble sound in the throat is produced that others can hear and may think is the voice of the heart as it recites. But this is not the case. I myself have heard this and seen others react in this way.

Morsel 9

It may be that one is overcoming with longing to discover some divine secret, and this may be an impediment to one's spiritual advancement. If one's inner reality throws up such distractions, then one should turn to one's own spiritual guide with one's inner attention and in one's outer action, while observing all the norms of respectful conduct. If the spiritual guide perceives one's spiritual plight and knows how to solve it, he might inform one of this directly or through some metaphor. Or winking, he might just say, "The time has not yet arrived for you to discover such a secret!"

Morsel 10

The goal of meditation is for one's self to be obliterated in the object of meditation. So do not intend to simply recite the name of God with the tongue or the heart. Remind yourself, "Although this may seem beneficial to me, yet I will never achieve the goal without being in the presence of the object of meditation." The goal of meditation is for one's self to be obliterated in the object of meditation—that is God—rather than being obliterated in merely the name of the object of meditation. Do not let the name distract from the presence.

Morsel 11

When one achieves connection with the vibration of recitation, one experiences many strange states and wondrous inspirations. One of these marvels is that one hears recitation from all things, even if this awareness comes gradually. One should not be arrested by this phenomenon, for the ultimate goal lies beyond this.

There is a subtle point that one must understand at this stage, so that one does not get confused. When one is engaged in reciting the name of God (Allah) with the heart, one might hear other things reciting the name of God, such as the wilderness or the walls, the room, or the stones. One might hear even one's hand or foot reciting the name of God! This is due to the one meditating being overcome with the power of one's own recitation. It is not due to the fact that other things are actually also reciting. Secondly, it is true that all things that exist have a special recitation though which it meditates on God. Most scholars think that this recitation is a spiritual state (*hali*) that is particular to any particular thing, but others think that this recitation is what each thing actually says (*maqali*). So think about it. Each thing existing is different and so is characterized by a distinctive kind of recitation through which it meditates on God. Every species and every type of thing is engrossed in a distinctly appointed way of reciting. The differentiation of things requires a differentiation in their existential recitations. It might be tenable that while one is meditating by reciting the name of God, one might hear other things—like the wall or the door or the prayer carpet—reciting each in their own distinctive way. But to hear everything reciting the same way that one recites the name of God? That is untenable.

Morsel 12

After arriving at this furthest stage and lofty station, it may sometimes happen that while intensely concentrating on the heart, a vibration can be felt in the flesh of the heart (*madgha*) and in the arteries (*shiryanat*). This vibration is distinct from the first in its quality. The first has distinct pulses that start and stop, while the second is continuous. The first is like the sound of "*Hu...Hu...*" which repeats in succession, while the second one is like that of "*Hu-u-u...,*" that is extended and continuous. The first vibration is like the sound of raindrops falling from high above and striking the ground in repeated pulses, with the sound of the falling and the sound of striking the ground being different. The second vibration is like the sound of a sheet of water pouring down from a height in one continuous motion without discrete drops of water being separable from others. The first vibration is like the sound of a hammer striking on an anvil with successive beats, and the second vibration is like that of a brass gong that is struck once and resounds with a continuous expansive sound.

One should disregard whether the first type of vibration is stronger or weaker than the second. Suffice it to say that the second type of vibration is subtler in comparison with the first. For this reason, it is felt only after long practice. It should be understood that the seeker can sense the first type of vibration which starts and stops when reciting names like God (Allah), True One (*haqq*), He (*hu*) or other such name, because each name has a particular sound that has a beginning and end.

So each name that has a beginning and end can generate the awareness of this first type of vibration that has discrete pulses. But the second vibration is continuous and singular without having any beginning or ending. So how could it be produced by reciting words and names whose sounds have beginning and end? This second type of vibration should be attributed to the object of meditation, namely God, rather than to the means of meditation, namely God's names, as is done with the first vibration. In the first case, God is the object of meditative search with names and words, while in the second case, God is the realization of that meditation. This explanation I have heard from some Sufi masters, may God be content with them.[45]

A detailed explanation of this is as follows. You may say, "The object of meditation and search (namely God) is characterized by the quality of being absolute, but the quality of being absolute is indeed limited by being a quality. Such a thing that has qualities cannot be truly absolute. Something is absolute by its being unqualified by any limited thing, not by its being qualified by nothingness. Thus when the seeker is aware of a vibration of the second type, he is still aware of something in the phenomenal world of sensory perception. So how can this vibration be attributed to God? Tell me if I am right or wrong!" I would answer that a thing that is related to absoluteness is nearer and closer to being absolute than something which is related to limitation. Therefore, since the second type of vibration is more absolute in its existence than the first type of vibration which is relative and limited, it shares more of the quality of the object sought which is absolute, namely God. That said, we can admit that both types vibration are

45. Beck, *Sonic Theology,* 206 writes that "The identification of absolute and unqualified being with both God and with the sound-vibration is common to Hindu speculation and Sufi thought in India. In a way, it requires the use of language-as-sound to transcend language itself, as a network of symbols that structures cognition and roots self-identification. This explains the use of language-as-sound (rather than language-as-speech) in mysticism as a vehicle of meditation."

of the existent world (*'alam-i tanazzulat*) and both are manifestations of divine names and qualities. If one continues to cultivate these practices, with time it will become clear what is obliterated in obliteration and what is sustained in sustenance. This is the furthest goal.

Now I round out this point by recounting a story. In my youth, one day I went to a spiritual master in order to learn the right way and the straight path. Before this point, I was always engrossed in devotional exercises. In fact, my devotions became so intense that I was left with a spiritual thirst that no devotion could quench. The master thought deeply and then said, "It is suitable for you now to be engrossed now in the eternal sound *(sawt-i sarmadi)* also known as the everlasting sound (*sawt-i la-yazali*), which is known amongst Yogins as the unstruck sound *(anahad)*." I replied, "I will do so, if you would confer this teaching to me." He then told me, "Firmly close the holes of both ears with your forefingers. Then concentrate and listen within your mind for a sound that resembles the sound of water continuously falling from on high. Turn your entire concentration to listening for this sound and do not be distracted from hearing it for even a moment. When you become proficient in listening to this sound then withdraw your fingers from your ear bit by bit. As you do this, continue to concentrate on hearing it such that even in the world's din you are not absent from this sound. Gradually, you must reach the stage where you hear this inner sound even without stopping up your ears with your fingers and never be disrupted by the distracting clamor of the world and worldly people. Rather, the eternal sound will overwhelm you regardless of all other external noises. In this state, you will feel bliss that is beyond words to describe." Some people stuffed their ears with black pepper rolled in cotton, so that the heat generated by the pepper might make this sound more powerfully heard. But I heard from others that they tied string around the pepper to pull it out easily. Once it is stuffed into the ear it can be very hard to remove. Others wrap the pepper in a small piece of red silk so that the heat generated by the pepper is even more and the sound heard might be more intense. The pepper so used for a year is effective as a remedy for eye-diseases.

When the spiritual master ceased speaking, I closed my ears with the fingers as I was told. Truly, I heard a murmuring resonance just like he had described. For a while I concentrated on this sound. I felt something in me that had not been there before. I turned to him and said, "Master, when will God remove the veil from the divine face? For that is what I seek and the stage of love is lower than that!" To this he said, "Miyan Mir of Lahore and his companions adopted the practice of listening for this eternal sound which they called "the divine presence (*hazrat-i haqq*.)" At that time I was a student and was spending all my time learning from books and was only a beginner on the spiritual path, so I was very sad to hear these words. At that time, I spurned this practice with disdain.

But later I came to Medina, the blessed city that is lit up by the presence of the Prophet Muhammad. I arrived in the presence of my spiritual guide, Shaykh Yahya Madani, and told him of this event. He said, "This practice is very good and beneficial! It is practiced in common by both Muslim holy men and powerful ascetics of other religions."[46] The effect of doing this practice is that distracting thoughts as a whole are focused in one direction by one's high aspiration. The sound serves as a connection between the seeker and the One sought, namely God. It bestows upon one a state of selflessness and self-absence which is the beginning of obliteration of obliteration (*fana' al-fana'*). Those who claim that sound is the divine say this because the sound resembles God in its absolute and unconditioned quality, as implied by the verse in Qur'an that says, "There is nothing like unto God, for God is the One who

46. The text describes Muslim holy men as *sahib-i karamat* or those who perform miracles by God's grace. It describes powerful ascetics of others religions (namely Hindu Yogis) as *sahib-i istidraj* or those who perform wonders by their own penitence or sorcery. But the sense of the text is that both Muslim and Hindu holy men do this practice.

hears, who sees."[47] The relationship he drew between what is absolute and what is limited is just like that above, describing the relationship between the first type of vibration and the second type.

Morsel 13

When this second vibration, which is continuous and sustained, becomes known to the seeker, it begins to spread through the body part by part depending upon the purity of its constitution and the intensity of the vibration. Some people may feel this vibration in only one part of the body. In any case, the manifestation of this vibration should cause one to keep focusing upon God, the true goal. If one is unable to focus upon God, then one should concentrate upon the heart without conceiving of the word Allah or any divine name. If it is difficult to focus upon God without conceiving of any divine name, then one should do this through conceiving of a divine name. But at this stage, focusing only upon a divine name without realizing the reality signified by the name is very detrimental. To turn back to a later stage when one has progressed to a more advanced stage is infidelity! As the proverb says, "The good deeds of the righteous appear as sins to the spiritually realized."[48]

The perception of the vibration is quantitatively equal to the vibration itself. In other words, the extent of perception should increase with the intensity of the vibration. I can offer these tricks in order to help the seeker increase this perception, for dependent upon this perception are reward and punishment, intimacy or distance, presence or estrangement. Since the source of both kinds of vibration is the heart, one is helped to perceive the vibration by concentrating on the heart rather than on any other part of the body. Observe that concentrating on any part of the body except the heart means concentrating less on other parts of the body. But this is not the case with the

---

47. Surat al-Shura 42:11 which says *Laysa ka-mithli-hi shay wa huwa 'l-sami' al-basir.*

48. This proverb in Arabic is: *"Hasanat al-abrar sayi'at al-muqaribin."*

heart. Concentrate on the heart, for concentrating on it means also concentrating on all other parts of the body. At this moment, three things are in complete accord and conjunction: first, the vibration throughout the entire body, and second, the object of meditation which is denoted by the name Allah and the reality that it connotes, and third, knowledge of the object of meditation. One then realizes the vibration and time itself, which otherwise come under the category of phenomenal object that are conditioned and limited. At this stage, one is overwhelmed by an onslaught of self-abnegation and unself-consciousness, and one is taken up into the state of obliteration of obliteration (*fana' al-fana'*).

Morsel 14

With much practice, one attains awareness of this vibration most all of the time. Then one should aspire to be aware of this vibration without the mediation of the heart. One should focus upon it so intensely that one is not even aware of the heart. One should advance to the stage in which both the heart and the vibration are transcended. One should be aware of nothing but the object of meditation, namely God. Accord with any other thing should be discarded. Absence of duality is gained by singularity of focus that dissolves all conception of duality. We only imagine a dualism that separates knowledge and the object of meditation, that separates knowledge and the vibration which is known. One must have high aspiration to cultivate this relationship, which begins as little and proceeds towards much, and advances from much towards always and ever. In some moments one may not be able to maintain this relationship with the absolute directly, without any medium, due to some weakness. Then one should search out that vibration and concentrate upon it without any delay. If one gets distracted from maintaining contact with the continuous, universal vibration of the entire body, then one should concentrate instead on the continuous particular vibration of the heart. If that is also lost, one should concentrate on the periodic particular vibration of the heart. If that is also lost, one gathers one's concentration again by taking a cold bath or, if that is not practical, by breathing in two or three times with force until the breath reaches the head. Or else one can recite in the heart the divine name "One who does" (*faʿal*) several times, while keeping in mind the meaning of the name, for this will remove all obstacles that cause one to be misled, if God wills.

Morsel 15

With long practice and divine grace, one can reach the stage where one is constantly in the divine presence of the one meditated upon without struggling to concentrate on the continuous universal vibration of the entire body. Then, one should be careful not to be distracted from it even for a moment, no matter what one is doing with the limbs or in the heart. At this stage, one can be said to "Keep your hands busy with work and your heart engaged with the beloved."[49] As it is said in this quatrain:

My brother, the sources of richness always tend
Don't let this life towards distraction bend
At all times, wherever you are, whatever you do
Keep your heart's gaze secretly on your friend

sar-i rishta-yi daulat, ay baradar, bi-kaf ar
wa-in ʿumr-i giran-maya bi-ghaflat ma-guzar
daʾim hame ja ba hame kas dar hame kar
mi-dar nihufta chashm-i dil janib-i yar

Morsel 16

Concentration upon God, the object of meditation, without any intermediary is a great and precious achievement. When this happens, one has realized the true meditation of the heart.

49. This proverb in Persian reads: *"Dast bi-kar o dil bi-yar."*

As long as one is concentrating through an intermediary (like the vibrations) it is not meditation of the heart. This is because the heart is a subtle energy center (*latifa*) that is of God. Some even say that the heart does not belong to the body or corporeal organs. Some sages claim that the heart is actually a power of awareness, and others opine that it is an existence unconditioned by material limitations. Some think the heart is a subtle vapor. Some consider the heart to come directly from divine command, while others think that it belongs to the world of phenomena. Most agree that the heart is a divine essence, but some hold that it is incapable of definition. I have given a full account of these in my book *Those Ten Complete Days* (*Tilka 'Ashara Kamila*), including the heart (*qalb*), the soul (*nafs*), the spirit (*ruh*) and the intellect (*'aql*).[50] The vibration that one senses is part of the phenomenal world, and this is very far from the spiritual nature of the heart itself.

Morsel 17

When meditation of the heart is attained, then light begins to manifest to the seeker, sometimes from within the self and sometimes from without. For instance, light could manifest in the heart or the head, or in the right or the left hand, and these states are all praiseworthy. Or light could manifest from throughout the entire body which is an extraordinary rare event. As for light manifesting from without, it could appear from one's right side or from the left side, from above or from the front, and these are also all praiseworthy states. Full detail about these various kinds of light have already been noted above in a previous morsel.

50. Shaykh Kalimullah here refers to his book in Arabic entitled *Those Ten Complete Days* (*Tilka 'Ashira Kamila*). He wrote this little book by collecting the sayings of previous Sufi masters on essential spiritual topics, one for each day of the last ten days of Ramadan, the month of fasting. It is a custom to spend these ten days alone in isolated prayer, and Kalimullah did this in October 1681 CE (Ramadan 1092 AH), and during those ten complete days he wrote this book for his own benefit and that of others.

The essential point is that the seeker should not stay in this stage and long for the appearance of such light. One can traverse the spiritual path successfully without ever experiencing the manifestation of such light, and there is great hope that such a person can reach the goal even faster. So although the manifestation of light is a great blessing, one should strive towards having one's knowledge of the light come without any why or how so as to maintain the proper relationship between one's knowledge, what one knows, and one's ultimate goal. The goal is comprehending God in an absolute way without having any limitation of how or attachment to forms.

This may be explained in the following way. The seeker discovers a relation to the ultimate goal, which is God, that is felt like a cord. One end of the cord is from the center of the heart and the other end of the cord is attached to the divine essence. But the divine essence, is absolute and unqualified by limitation of time, space and condition, so it is impossible for a cord to be attached to it which is qualified by limitations. Nothing can be attached to such an essence unless it becomes a command of the absolute (*amr-i mutlaq*), that is, unqualified by a limitation in its essence unqualified by questions of more or less or how or why. Seekers who are not experts in the rational sciences (like mathematics or philosophy) may get upset when trying to imagine this kind of abstract schema. But those who, by love of science and learning, have trained their intellects will experience no anxiety in trying to conceive of this with force of imagination.

Yes, one must put up with some discomfort and tediousness! In the beginning, one may experience no delight in striving to be attached with such a cord as a command of the absolute that is beyond limitation in any dimension. In fact, one might count it completely futile and a waste of precious time! But with the help of love and the power of longing and desire to traverse these spiritual stations, the seeker can overcome this boredom and dedicate himself to this work.

Soon the seeker gets experience and this imagination gets perfected, and then he begins to know his true nature. Sufi masters advise seekers in this station not to do too much of conventional devotions, like reciting formulas (*wird*) or reading litanies (*wazifa*) or making supererogatory prayers (*nawafil*), for this might cause one's hold on the cord to be lost. For seekers who are having trouble making the connection to this command of the absolute, some Sufi masters recommend that they concentrate upon the entire cosmos without paying attention to any of its specific features and stripping away its distinctive aspects. For after ignoring the features and stripping away the distinctions in the cosmos, nothing is left except the absolute essence of existence (*itlaq-i hayulani*).

Some interpret this absolute to be like an ocean of light (*darya-yi nur*) and conceive the self to be a tiny droplet of light that dissolves into that vast ocean of light. Some assert that this absolute is like an endless darkness and think of the self as a shadow that is obliterated in the black expanse. Some state that this absolute is the ether that is between and connects the heavens and the earth and all existing things. All these are metaphors through which reason uses sensory data to approximate a reality that it cannot be directly described. Thus understand the people endowed with reason through the paltry means available to our unreceptive minds; truly God is above any such comparison or metaphor, yet people need diverse ways to attain what they love. The true aim is for each person to obliterate his phantasmal existence (*ifna-yi hasti-yi mawhum*) which obscures him from bearing witness to the absolute being which is his true reality. All these constitute ways and means to attain this lofty essence which we seek.

One experiences obliteration (*fana'*) when spiritual experiences overcome one's knowledge of one's own individual existence—no, not only knowledge of one's own self but also knowledge of anything other than the self! When one no longer has knowledge of the self and also has no knowledge of this knowledge, then one experiences obliteration of obliteration (*fana'-yi fana'*). In as much as one leaves behind one's self, one gains intimate connection to the absolute, which is God, as expressed in this poetic line:

> As much as I leave myself behind, I find myself
> in your embrace
>
> *An qadr ke az khweshtan raftam dar aghosh-tu-am*

In short, the seeker finds a certain relationship within his or her cognitive self (*nafs-i natiqa*) but the seeker does not know to what this relationship is connected on the other side. For anything to which there can be a connection is necessarily bound by existential specificity (*ta'ayyun*) that limits it, but the divine presence that is desired and sought is necessarily beyond specificity that limits. Whatever level of understanding the seeker may attain, the divine presence is beyond that. Whatever comes within the grasp of the understanding and imagination of the seeker is thereby specified and limited. It is limited by being within the imagination of the seeker.

Every existing thing exists by its specificity and its individualization, which are necessarily limited, so such things cannot possibly be the divine presence that is sought. For this reason, some sages have said that no saint or prophet has ever attained the essence of the divine.

> The phoenix cannot be captured
> so pull back your net
> As you search for the phoenix
> keep firmly in hand your net

Thus the seeker knows that "I am turning my concentration towards the divine, but I do not know to which direction I am turning my concentration." Thus the seeker does not know what he knows. This level of comprehension is called obliteration (*fana'*).

And if the seeker knows that he knows that he does not know, and goes beyond that to not know that he knows anything, then this level of comprehension is called obliteration of obliteration (*fana' al-fana'*). This level is the furthest that one can attain in the journey towards God (*sayr ila 'llah*). Beyond it lies journeying in God (*sayr fi 'llah*).

Morsel 18

What we call obliteration (*fana'*) is of two kinds. The first kind is a type of compound knowledge (*'ilm-i murakkab*) while the second is essential knowledge (*'ilm-i basit*). Compound knowledge is an expression that means a kind of comprehending that originates within the seeker and extends outward to concentrate upon the divine presence, thereby disengaging from everything that is other than the divine and attaching itself to nothing other than the divine.

This could be because everything he apprehends he does not conceive as other, but rather conceives it as essential to himself; though they may be clothed in the appearance of other things, he apprehends them all to not be existing other than as part of his own existence. One should know that this apprehension is actual and is in accord with reality. This is the belief of those who hold to the school of "The Unity of Being" (*wahdat-i wujud*) in a pure way and clean themselves of the dust of otherness. Or this could be because everything he apprehends he sees as his beloved, because of his intense concentration on his goal, his extreme seeking for his desired one, his overwhelming love for his friend, and his powerful passion for his lover. But one should know that this apprehension is not in accord with reality. For in reality, the multitude of existing things other than God actually come from the special divine presence that is the one necessary being (*wajib al-wujud*); but due to excessive yearning, they were made apparent as other than God. So the statement that "All is God" (*hame u-st*) is a misleading statement that is not in accord with reality. Those who really believe in "The Unity of Being" see this statement as immature. But both groups are in agreement that one should disregard things other than God, because of their otherness, in order to achieve apprehension of unity.

Thus the seeker flees from knowing the many and takes refuge in knowledge of the one. With this act of making the many one (*tawhid*), he finds intimacy with God. But still there remains the fact that he knows this knowledge. Because he is the knower, his knowledge remains a kind of compound knowledge—his knowledge is still derived from knowledge of something other.

As long as you hold to the thought that you exist
In the field of the idol worshippers you subsist
You say, "I believe in breaking idols, so I'm free."
You're mistaken! the idol of self you have missed

ta dar tu pindar-i tu hasti baqi-st
maidan-i baqin ke but-parasti baqi-at
gufti but pindar shikastam rast-am
in but ke tu pindar shikasti baqi-st

Such is the meaning of compound knowledge, the first type of knowledge. The second type is essential knowledge (*ʿilm-i basit*). This is an expression for a type or kind of comprehending which consists of turning one's concentration towards the divine presence, by which the seeker gets disengaged from everything else until even awareness of this knowledge also does not remain. In this state, the knowledge of the seeker is essential knowledge, and the seeker attains true obliteration (*fanaʾ-i haqiqi*). In the opinion of some sages, the first type—compound knowledge of the divine—is called obliteration (*fanaʾ*), and the second type—essential knowledge of God—is called obliteration of obliteration (*fanaʾ-i fanaʾ*). Both kinds of knowledge are not acquired by one's own effort. Rather they are bestowed by blessed emanation of the holiest divine majesty, without the efforts of the seeker having any influence upon it.

Nobody attains the goal by their own searching
Yet without searching nobody ever attains the goal

bi-justaju'i na-yabad kasi murad wali
kasi murad bi-yabad ke justaju bi-konad

Only after extreme longing, being pulled by divine attraction, experiencing unselfconsciousness and attaining self-absence, it may be that someone receives this blessed gift, after persisting for a long time thinking that, despite all entreaties, he is receiving nothing. Without the seeker going through a long period of divine attraction and unselfconsciousness, he can never have the quality of being intimate with God (*wilayat*). Yet without these, he can still be considered among the strict ascetics, pious devotees, righteous worshippers and virtuous persons, though he may not have that closeness to union which is the essential meaning of intimacy.

You should know that being pulled by divine attraction (*jazba*) is a necessary condition for becoming a saint. But having this state of divine attraction last for a long time—or forever—is not a condition for being a saint. It sometimes happens that a person may be pulled by the divine (*majzub*) and act intoxicated for many years, but then later be sent back to his senses. They say this was the case with Bayazid Bistami, the Sultan of Sages, who for thirty years was in a state of intoxication and self-absence. But it could be that one experiences this for just a moment, and that is sufficient. But one who stays in a state of divine attraction and senselessness (*majzub*) is limited by this and does not progress beyond this stage, for without coming to one's senses one cannot be worthy of giving spiritual training (*tarbiyat*). But the Sufi masters—who are the kings who sit on the throne of awareness, and who serve as the vice-regents of the Prophets, may God grant them peace and blessing—are able to dispense this spiritual treasure to others.

Morsel 19

Being sustained through God (*baqa' bi'llah*) is an expression meaning "being concentrated into unity" (*jam' al-jam'*), which confers an intense bewilderment (*hayrat-i kubra).* Most sages of this age hold that this great bewilderment is the ultimate station (*maqam*) of the spiritual path, but others hold that the ultimate station is contentment (*riza'*) and acceptance (*taslim*).

Being sustained through God means returning to the beginning (*ruju' illa 'l-bidayat*). The beginning is the state of having one's attention dispersed and apprehending the multitude of various things as individual and separate existences. Yet one returns to the beginning while disregarding the vision of a beginning and proceeding to apprehend phenomenal appearances without taking them merely as they appear. In this station, one has undergone an utter distraction that overpowers one's spiritual condition and then, after progressing to the zenith of self-absence and unselfconsciousness—in which one is pulled towards the divine by uncontrollable attraction, discards all fetters, disregards all boundaries, and eradicates all specificities and dependencies—then one returns to the state of considering the multitude of existing things and separate identities and conditioned beings. But one returns to the beginning with a different vision, not with the vision of a beginner!

These two stations share certain common features, even if one's vision is different within them. Both are similar in that one regards the multitude of separate existing things. Yet there is a great difference between them! In the beginning state, the seeker's heart is searching for and longing for and concentrating on God, while it is limited by the various existing things with their separate identities, and does not observe and realize the command of the absolute (*amr-i mutlaq*). However, in the other state, the seeker's heart is searching for and longing for and concentrating on God as the absolute essence (*zat-i mutlaq*), such that all separate identities, conditioned beings and individual existences are seen to be manifestations of the divine names (*asma'*) and qualities (*sifat*). Just as in the first state, the seeker distinguishes between lovely phenomena (*jamal*) and wrathful phenomenon (*jalal*), so also in the second state he distinguishes between them but with an eye transformed and a vision altogether different.

In the second state, some say that when they observe existing things and apparent phenomena, they first bear witness to the absolute essence and then, by the light of that essence, they see the multitude of individual existing things and conditioned beings. Others say that they bear witness to the absolute essence in seeing the multitude of phenomenal appearances. And yet others say that one can bear witness to the absolute essence only after observing the multitude of phenomenal things. It is as if the first one says, "I do not see anything unless I see God before it," while the second says, "I do not see anything unless I see God within it," while the third one says, "I do not see anything unless I see God after it."[51] I submit to you the proverb, "Each of us has a specific station that is known to him."[52]

When in the end a spiritual master returns to the routine world in this way, common people have difficulty recognizing him and distinguishing him from others. In this regard, you should understand why God says, "My friends are concealed under my cloak and no one knows them except for me."[53] Upon this foundation, you can now understand why the words of some blind persons, in deriding the Prophet Muhammad

51. In Arabic, these sayings are: *Ma ra'aytu shay'an illa wa-ra'aytu 'llaha qabla-hu. Ma ra'aytu shay'an illa wa-ra'aytu 'llaha fi-hi. Ma ra'aytu shay'an illa wa-ra'aytu 'llaha ba'da-hu.* These sayings are frequently quoted by Ibn 'Arabi, for example in *al-Futuhat al-Makkiya,* vol. 2 in chapter 126 entitled "*ma'rifat maqam al-muraqaba.*"

52. In Arabic, this saying is: "*ma minna illa wa la-hu maqam ma'lum.*"

53. This is a hadith qudsi, a report from Muhammad which relates the saying of God. In Arabic, the saying is: "*Awliya'i tahta qaba'i la ya'rifuhum ghayri.*" See Schimmel, *Mystical Dimensions of Islam,* 203.

(on whom be peace), are cited in the Qur'an, saying "What is with this man who claims to be a Prophet yet eats common food and walks in the marketplace?"[54] Another verse of Qur'an refers to people in the station, when it says, "Men who are not distracted with buying and selling from the remembrance of God."[55]

Thus you can see that it is difficult to recognize the true people of God who have realized this ultimate station of spiritual development. This is because their appearance and behavior is like that of ordinary people. In contrast, those who are distracted by the divine (*majzub*) and those mad for God (*majnun*), whose behavior and appearance are so different from that of ordinary people, are easily recognized by others and readily believed in by them. But among the rational and sensible people, those few who have returned from a station of spiritual uniqueness (*fardiyat haqiqiya*) do nothing unusual, and seldom do miracles happen with them. This is because they focus their full concentration on the absolute essence that is so pure as to be devoid of all qualities, while miraculous acts in this world and the cosmos are effects of divine qualities (*sifat*). They have moved above and beyond that state in which miraculous acts would appear from them. The details of this ultimate station are beyond words and description, as it says in the Qur'an, "Say 'If the ocean were ink for writing the words of my Lord, the ocean would finish before the words of my Lord would finish, even if another ocean like it were added to help!'"[56]

Oh my brother, if you read these meager lines with an attentive heart, there is a great hope your effort might move from the lowest depth to reach the loftiest apex even without a spiritual guide. But I know well that without the attention of a spiritual guide, this effort does not reach perfection. There are so many obstacles which can be surmounted only with the

54. Surat al-Furqan 25:7.
55. Surat al-Nur 24:37.
56. Surat al-Kahf 18:109.

inner help of a spiritual guide, and such aid is impossible to get by the mere reading of books.[57]

Some vain and self-conceited people do not wish to take initiation from any spiritual guide or keep their company, yet desire that through books alone they might learn about meditation and contemplation and have their spiritual effort reach perfection! This is nearly impossible and unthinkably rare. "Oh Lord, decide between us and our people in truth, for you are the best of all who decide!"[58]

General Advice

Morsel 1

You should know, and may God guide you to the truth, that the object of all these types of meditation, reflection and contemplation is for you to be effaced and to strip away worldly concerns. This may reveal to you the true grandeur and subtlety of God. For the nature of one who realizes the singleness of God is of firm resolve and concentrated unity, and he strengthens his connection to the true source of the universe. Then from that state of being concentrated and resolved, he arrives back into the world of difference and separation. So a person with lofty aspiration and keen sense of justice always aims to turn towards that sense of unity. As much as he dispenses with what is dispersed and separate he achieves a strong bond with divine unity. And there is no way to achieve this except to render the knowledge of yourself as essential knowledge, and thereby disregard directions of the many and turn your face towards the one, until you see no essence in the whole world except the

---

57. About these obstacles, Shaykh Kalimullah has written another small book in Arabic entitled *Essentials of Kalimullah* (*Ma La Budda Kalimi*) in which he details ten such spiritual obstacles, which he completed in 1662–63 CE (1073 AH).

58. Surat al-Aʿraf 7:89. This prayer recalls the words of the Prophet Shuʿayb as cited in the Qurʾan.

divine essence and perceive no qualities except divine qualities and acknowledge no actions except divine actions.

Such a person comes to know the secret that permeates his very existence which also courses within every other being in existence. In this state, he achieves true faith (*iman*) and perfect awareness of God (*taqwa*). It is revealed to him what is heaven and what is hell. He realizes what is this world and what is the world to come. He comprehends what is the spirit and what is the soul. He understands who is the tempter and who is the compassionate. He apprehends who guides truly and who leads astray. Although the mystic sage has no goal to discover all these things, he is impelled to bear witness to them.

The ways of doing meditation, reflection and contemplation are all based on love (*'ishq*). The greater one's love the greater is the effect of all these practices. But if love is lax then their effect is lesser. These different types of spiritual practices might aid one to restore the strength and intensity of love that sometimes lags and weakens. One should never do these practices of meditation, reflection and contemplation merely to get some reward. A true lover's aspiration is surely loftier than that.

Morsel 2

You will observe that all the varieties of meditation that have been detailed above involve pronouncing words that assert the unity of God (*tawhid*). Likewise, there are poems and couplets composed in every age that express the unity of God. For this reason, reciting such poems is useful in striving to achieve union with the divine, and especially effective are those in the Arabic language which praise the more complete manifestation of prophethood (Muhammad), may God bless him and grant him peace. The effect of these poems is especially strong, though poems in any language that reveal the prophetic reality are useful.

What does love have to do with believer or infidel?
You can write this verse in either mosque or temple!

ʿIshq ra ba kafir o mumin na-bashad ihtiyaj
In sukhan dar masjid o but-khana mi-bayad navisht

Morsel 3

Spiritual guides in the Sufi way have established the principle of focusing on a "medium" (*barzakh*) as a means whereby the dispersed attention can be gathered in concentrated unity. The human being has the attention dispersed through the various senses and is plagued by a host of distracting thoughts and is thus prevented from apprehending the true knowledge of divine unity (*tawhid*). Therefore, focusing attention upon a medium is a means to gather into unity all the senses and thoughts. This is particularly so when the medium is someone who commands reverence and demands respectful behavior.

By focusing on the image of one's spiritual guide, whether in real vision or in imagination, this medium serves to demand attention and respect, and in his presence one naturally exhibits awe and modesty. This is most useful. With much practice, the meaning that is inherent in the medium of one's spiritual guide's form becomes apparent within the seeker himself. This is so because thought takes on the color of whatever it reflects upon, just like material objects reflect what is near them. Likewise, the human being is capable of taking on the quality of any form that is dear to him, as expressed in this line from Maulana Rumi's *Masnavi*:

My brother, of thoughts entirely you are composed
Though bone and hair remain after you're decomposed
If you think of roses, your life is a garden amazing
If you think of thorns, your life is a furnace blazing

Ay baradar, tu hamin andeshaʾi
ma baqi tu ustukhwan o reshaʾi

gar gul-ast andesha tu gulshani
war bud khari tu hame gulkhani

Any existing thing can function as a medium, because the term *medium* means something that serves as an intermediary (*wasita*) between a person's heart and the sought-for divine. But since the divine is of an extremely subtle and transcendent nature, it cannot be grasped by the senses or intellect. For this reason, the beauty of the divine is made present through the intermediary of the medium. From the smallest speck of dust to the radiant sphere of the sun, from the lowest earth to the loftiest heavens, everything is a place of manifestation (*jalwa-gah*) of the divine. The more subtle in nature the thing chosen as a medium, and the more profound its meaning for the intellect, the more intense is its effect. The more gross in nature the thing chosen as a medium, and the further it is from the human form, the less intense is its effect. Wherever you may look, if you look with the eye of wisdom and discernment, you see the divine essence. Yet what one chooses as a medium makes a big difference. Taking as a medium the form of one's spiritual guide engenders a different symbolic meaning, which would be very different from that engendered by taking a stone or a clod of mud as a medium.

The Sufi masters used to choose for each disciple a medium that suits his or her nature. For a disciple with a strong intellect, one would chose something abstract and universal from the realm of rational meanings. For a disciple who is weaker in intellect, one would chose some objects or image that is sensory and specific. But the master would chose a medium only after careful consideration of the internal state of the disciple, as to what thing he or she values most and is most beautiful in his or her sight. For example, consider someone who is in love with a young man and is mad with passion for him. He would feel that the beauty of this young man is more intense than that of his spiritual guide. So when the spiritual guide decides what should serve as the medium for him, he would chose the image of that young man whom he loves. Gradually, after long practice with these many meditations and contemplations, he would be released from this trap, as his relation to physical things lessens and his relation to spiritual things deepens. Take, for example, a person who feels that a rose in the garden is more beautiful than anything else. The medium for him would be the image of this rose. For if his spiritual guide would command that his own form serve as the medium for his man, it would not serve the purpose as well as this rose would. Then after these meditative practices, he would slowly be released from this obsession with roses and move on to higher things.

Morsel 4

The various kinds of meditation that involve forceful motion are to engender an internal heat within the practitioner that increases the feeling of passion, engenders yearning and stokes the fires of love. These kinds that demand strain and effort include suspending the breath or restraining the breath, or the meditation in two beats, the meditation in six beats, or the meditation of the blacksmith. In performing meditations like these, the seeker should feel impassioned and should call out in ecstasy. For this reason, it is said that teaching the youth these kinds of meditations bears fruit more quickly. It is said that the Sufi after thirty years becomes cool and frigid. One should not teach these kinds of meditation to children who have not reached the age of maturity, lest they burn up with the internal heat it generates. When they reach the age of adolescence, then they may do it. The ardors that youthful years can endure cannot be borne by those in old age. The visions and unveilings achieved by the young cannot be attained by the aged. Shaykh Nizam al-Din Narnauli gave a prescription for older seekers who feel cool.[59] He suggested they consume the seeds

59. Shaykh Nizam al-Din Narnauli was a master who died in 1589 at Narnaul (a town in Haryana in North India). He was a disciple of Khwaja Qanun, a famous Chishti Sufi of Gwalior during the early Mughal period. The

of Panwar plant for the purpose of generating internal heat and stimulating motion in their constitutions by means of an herbal remedy.[60]

Morsel 5

There is a secret in the practice of devotions and meditations that involves the beating of the heart, hearing the eternal sound (*sawt-i sarmadi*) and sequence of breaths. The secret is in their constantly repeating nature. These practices are perfected with constant repetition, and when perfected they also repeat continuously. Their constantly repeating nature is a fundamental feature that can be found in other phenomena in the cosmos. For example, observe the motion of the heavenly bodies and stars that are in constant perpetual motion, or the movement of waves in the ocean. But such phenomena are external to the human body and so they are difficult for us to focus upon. It is easier for us to focus on the constant repetition and perpetual motion that is existent without our own human bodies, such as the beating of the heart or the oscillating of the breath. You may object by saying, "Every moment the human being is changing color and mood and yet the human being remains the same over time, so why don't we consider the outer form of the human body as the principle of constant perpetual motion?" I would reply, "First of all, color is dependent upon the eye that sees it. In contemplations and even in meditation, closing the eyes is not just beneficial but rather essential. Secondly, its constant renovation is not self-evident but is rather only a

---

Mughal Emperor Akbar visited Nizam al-Din Narnauli, as narrated by the historian Nizam al-Din Ahmad in *Tarikh-i Alfi*; see Henry Elliot, *The History of India as Told by its Own Historians,* vol. 7 page 407. Narnaul is also the location of the dargah of Shaykh Muhammad Turkman Narnauli who was a disciple of Shaykh Usman Harwani, the spiritual guide of Muʿin al-Din Chishti.

60. Panwar in Hindi is the name of a shrub that grows in Northern India with the scientific name *Cassia Tora*, commonly called "Sickle Senna" or "Wild Senna" or "Coffee Pod Tree" that is used in Ayurvedic medicine and is sometimes used as a stimulant and coffee substitute.

matter of opinion. It would take some surgical experiments to establish for certain that this is the truth."

Morsel 6

A melody is a fiery spark in the seeker's heart that is kindled by intense love. It is not something external to the seeker that affects him within. In the beginning, listening to music causes weeping and lamenting and restlessness and violent movements and moisture in the eyes, nose and mouth. These effects are due to the pain that is felt, a pain that is caused by performing much meditation. But those who have reached the station of bewilderment do not weep out of separation but rather they weep at the prospect of union. If they do weep, they do so because of regret for what is past or for some cause arising out of love. The tears of these, it is said, are sweet while those who weep from pain are bitter. Further, their movement in dancing is extremely soft, gentle and harmonious, and most often they dance in perfect accord with the rhythm of the melody. This motion is called "according to spiritual discourses" (*nawatiq-i ruhani*). It is enough to demonstrate their open-heartedness and expansive joyous spirit, though common people do not consider this kind of dance and movement very interesting. Common people like listening to music that causes forceful movement. But the spiritually attuned recognize where this subtle movement comes from, that is from the submissive prostration of the heart.

While people are listening to the music, the person who first gets up and begins to dance in ecstasy is responsible for whatever happens in the assembly, whether it is good or bad. Nizam al-Din Awliya says that if a Sufi's back touches the floor during such ecstasies, then he should sacrifice himself or give away one's clothes in charity. The author of the *Risala Qushayriya* says that while listening to music, movement of any sort diminishes the spiritual state of any seeker whether he is a beginner or advanced or in the middle.[61] It is therefore not proper for one to move from one's place no matter how overcome with emotion one might be. As far as possible, one should be firmly grounded and in control.

With this the writer closes this book. Even though there are many more things that should be said about meditation, there is nothing to be done about that. This book was finished on 3 October 1690 CE (the last day of Dhu'l-Hijja 1101 AH). Oh God, keep these pages safe from indolent seekers and idle listeners! So it is finished, by the sacredness of the leader of the pious and his most pure family and followers. May God grant peace and blessings to Muhammad along with his kith and kin.

61. Abu'l-Qasim al-Qushayri was an early Sufi master and hadith scholar who lived in Nishapur and died in 1074. He wrote one of the most influential treatises on Sufi practice (*al-risala al-qushayriyya fi' l-tasawwuf*). See Michael Sells (trans. and ed.), *Early Islamic Mysticism* (Mahwah, NJ: Paulist Press, 1996; The Classics of Western Spirituality Series Number 86), 112.

The Compass of Truth
by Dara Shikoh

Translator's Notes

by Scott Kugle

This is one of several compositions about Sufism by the Mughal prince Dara Shikoh. His other texts are about the lives of eminent Sufis of the past or about the complementarity of Hinduism and Islam, as seen through the lens of Sufism. In reality, this text represents his most intense engagement with Sufism. It describers both his concrete experience with meditation practices and the cosmological framework in which those meditation practices gain urgency and efficacy.

Dara Shikoh had in his personality a tendency towards mysticism, and his Mughal environment reinforced this, for it was founded on the ideal that Sufi guides of the past ensured the prosperity and success of his political rule. Earlier Mughal emperors had taken Shattari Sufis as their guides or patronized Chishti masters of the past. But Dara Shikoh, in his earnest zeal for mystical experience, found a spiritual guide in the Qadiri order, in the person of Mulla Shah. This treatise represents a true account of Dara Shikoh's training under Mulla Shah, and offers the reader intimate advice on how to meditate according to the Qadiri order's teachings in South Asia.

Dara Shikoh wrote this text in 1645 CE (1055 AH). Dara Shikoh was an ardent Qadiri Sufi. He wrote this text after having heard a voice of inspiration tell him that "the best possible way of reaching God was the Qadiri Sufi order." But his training in meditation techniques has much in common with the

Chishti Sufi order. Part of the value of this treatise is that it demonstrates the common basis of meditation techniques in both the Qadiri and Chishti Sufi orders. In the earliest printing of *Kashkul* in the lithograph edition used to render the translation in English offered above, the editor includes a note at the end giving a quote from *The Compass of Truth*. So the editor saw both of these as texts that were linked in their content.

This translation was rendered from a fine lithograph print. That print was published in October 1896 by Munshi Nawal Kishore Press in Lucknow, under the auspices of the Press's owner, Munshi Parag Narayan. It contains some useful marginal notes that were added by an editor to clarify certain ambiguities—especially in Arabic words or phrases that Indian readers of the Persian text might not immediately grasp.

In preparing this translation, I consulted an earlier English translation by Rai Bahadur Srisa Chandra Vasu made at the turn of the 20th century by a Bengali gentleman and lawyer (at the Northwest Province High Court) who appears to have been active in the Theosophical Movement. However, in referring back to the original Persian, I was dissatisfied with Vasu's earlier English translation, and ended up translating the text anew, adopting what was apt from the earlier translation but modifying it where improvements were needed. Improvements were necessary in the following cases: the original translation was not accurate, or was too abridged, or translated technical terms in a way inconsistent with other Sufi texts that use the same terms, or used a Victorian style of English that sounds outdated and precious to modern readers.

At the turn of the 20th century, it appears that Vasu was very active in translating mystical texts into English. He published an English translation of the *Shiva Samhita,* a Sanskrit text on Hatha Yoga; he published this translation as *The Esoteric Philosophy of the Tantra Shiva Sanhita* in 1887 in Calcutta, and dedicated the text to Henry Steel Olcott, an American colonel and early Buddhist convert who was the cofounder of the

Theosophical Movement with Madame Helena Blavatsky in 1875. On moving to India, Olcott and other Theosophical Society members sponsored a major drive to translate into English texts on "Eastern Spirituality," texts coming mainly from the Buddhist, Hindu, and Zoroastrian traditions; it appears that Srisa Chandra Vasu was one of the translators active during that optimistic age. These translations undoubtedly had a great effect on both Orientalist scholars and spiritual practitioners over the course of the 20th century, but as translations they are not totally firm and reliable. Vasu's translation of the *Shiva Samhita,* for instance, has been critiqued and laid aside by the contemporary scholar James Mallinson, as he prepared a new critical edition and translation of that text.[1]

As time moves on, scholarly knowledge grows and communication styles evolve, and so it is no insult to an intrepid translator from the past for a contemporary writer to retranslate a text. I appreciate the effort that Srisa Chandra Vasu put into translating *The Compass of Truth*, yet I did not rely upon his translation but rather went back to the Persian original in order to create a new translation that will be useful for modern readers. But for clarity, I should alert readers to just how this new translation differs from that done a century earlier. Here is an example of how my translation differs from the earlier English translation. Vasu wrote: "O friend! When thou shall begin to hear this voice, thou must attend to it very carefully and try to keep it with all thy might, so thou mayest be expert in hearing it; and may hear it not only in the solitude of the desert and the cloister, but in the bustle and noise of the market place, and meeting houses of mankind." I translated the same passage: "When this sound manifests to your hearing, my friend, you must observe it keenly. You must try your hardest

1. James Mallinson, *The Shiva Samhita* (Woodstock, NY: YogaVidya, 2007). On page xi, Mallinson acknowledges that Vasu's earlier translation was successful in securing the text a respected place among modern Yoga practitioners, but notes that the translation was in places inaccurate and abridged.

to preserve your ability to listen for it, until you can master it so that, just as you heard it in the silence of the wilderness or a closed room, you will also hear it in the noisy marketplace amid throngs of people."

I endeavored to use simpler language in a style that would be more immediately accessible to a contemporary reader. In addition, I was able to present how the text uses Arabic from the Qur'an, hadith reports, and other spiritual sources that Vasu did not fully grasp. Finally, I paid greater attention to systematically translating technical terms from the Sufi tradition into English, in a way that highlights the continuity between Dara Shikoh's text and others in the Sufi tradition. In contrast, Vasu had sometimes offered rather eccentric translations of technical terms based upon his prior philosophical commitments and the Theosophical Movement's eager universalism. With this caveat, I present to you *The Compass of Truth* by Dara Shikoh.

The Compass of Truth
by Dara Shikoh

In the name of God, the compassionate and merciful.

God is the first and the last, the manifest and the hidden.[1] Praise be to that divine essence who is the absolute existence (*mawjud-i mutlaq*). Reverence be to that prophet, to whom is revealed every thing and who is the vicegerent of the true One (*khalifa-i haqq*). Let profuse mercy shower on him, his descendants and his companions.

It is best that I not attempt to exhaustively do justice to their praise and reverence, so let me cut short this attempt, because whatever may be written on this point is bound to fall short of the truth. For the opinion of the sages (*arbab-i ʿirfan*) is that "No praise for you is sufficient, for you are as you have praised yourself!"[2]

So we turn to the point of this treatise. O friend, the reason why the human essence (*haqiqat-i insani*) has descended into this bodily frame (*haikal-i jismani*) is so the trust that was hidden as potential in it may become explicit and complete, so that it may return to its original source.

It is the duty of all human beings to struggle to save themselves from eternal loss, free themselves from the delusion of

1. Surat al-Hadid 57:3.
2. This saying in Arabic reads: *"la yuhsa thana ʿalayka, anta ka-ma athnayta ʿala nafsika."*

individual existence (*wahm-i ta'ayyunat*), and return to their true source. They should not waste this life, which lies as a flickering moment of time between the two eternities of past and future, in useless thoughts, words, and deeds. They must each save themselves from everlasting remorse and regret, and free themselves from eternal loss and ruin. They must strive to not be among those whom the Qur'an describes as "like dumb cattle—no, even more lost."[3] Indeed, they must not let go to waste that special and noble gift bestowed upon the human being in distinction from the rest of creation. That is the gift of reason and discrimination, for God says, "Surely we gave human beings a special endowment."[4] For God created the whole world for the sake of humanity, and created humanity especially for the sake of God. So each person must find a spiritual guide (*sahib-dil*) through whom to find release from the pain of loss and the pangs of separation, for one cannot find God without a dependable guide who has given up all else. Whoever has not given up the world (*faqr*) has not found God. And whoever has found God has given up the world. Though one might strive and struggle, this ultimate goal is one that is given undeserved rather than one that is earned and achieved.

Union can never be achieved by striving, that is right
Keep trying, O my heart, and strive with all your might

Gar-che visal-ash na bi-koshish dahand
An qadar ai dil keh tavani bi-kosh

There are two ways that one can reach presence of the holy One. The first is by bounty given undeserved (*fazl*). This means that God leads one to a spiritual guide who, with one glance and concentration, makes his spiritual condition complete. He raises the veil from his sight and wakes him up from the daze of

3. Surat al-Furqan 25:44.
4. Surat al-Isra 17:70.

negligence and opinion. He shows him the beauty of the divine beloved without any strain or struggle or difficulty. He releases him from the bonds of his ego and lets him rise to the exalted level of "by me, he hears, and through me, he sees."[5] As it says in the Qur'an, "This is the bounty of God who bestows it on those whom God wills, for God is the One with great bounty."[6]

The second way to reach God is through struggle (*mujahadat*) and exertion (*riyazat*). It happens in this way, that a man hears from others or reads in the sayings of previous times that certain persons have reached to God, and have known the true One with deep intuitive knowledge (*ma'rifat*) and have set off to reach union with that divine presence. This sparks in his mind a desire to reach the same lofty position. When this idea takes a strong hold on his heart, he begins to seek and search and engage in struggle and exertion by himself, till he finds a spiritual guide who can inform him about the path by which prior seekers of union have gone. Then he puts all his effort and struggle into following that path. And with all this, after countless labors and trials he might, if God grants divine bounty, he might catch sight of his goal and, by the blessing of those who have gone before him, his desire might be fulfilled.

The humble beggar at the court of the eternal One, named Muhammad Dara Shikoh who follows Hanafi law and the

5. This comes from a saying in which God says, "My servant draws near to me with nothing more beloved to me than duties which I have imposed. Then my servant continues to draw near to me with devotion beyond duty so that I love him. When I love him I become his hearing with which he hears, his seeing with which he sees, his doing with which he acts, and his ability with which he moves. Were he to ask something of me, I would surely give it to him, and were he to beseech me for refuge, I would surely grant it to him." This saying is one of the most famous hadith qudsi or saying of the Prophet Muhammad which interprets a message from God; it is recorded in al-Bukhari's *Sahih*.

6. Surat al-Ma'ida 5:54.

Qadiri Sufi order, belongs to that group of devotees who are attracted to God spontaneously without struggle or austerities. Through the glance of a spiritual guide, God has drawn him towards the divine and, by ceaseless grace, has shown him to the furthest goal. He has come to know all the levels of spiritual knowledge of divine unity in its subtleties and details. He has spent time in the company of most of the saints of his age. He has especially followed one of them who was exemplary in his era. He has stayed close to the blessed breaths of this spiritual guide, until he came to know through experience the desired goal shared by all the prophets and saints.

Then it was desirable to write an account of those dear saints in a book. So on a Friday, the 9th of September in the year 1645 (17 Rajab, 1055 AH), he heard a voice of inspiration which told him that the best possible way of reaching God was the Qadiri Sufi order. This order traces its origin back to the blessed Prophet and leader of humanity, Muhammad, of whom God said, "If not for you I would not have created the cosmos."[7]

It traces its origin back to him through the great leader of the sages, that sea of mystical knowledge and guide to God's people, Shaykh Muhyi al-Din ʿAbd al-Qadir Jilani, who once said, "This foot of mine is upon the neck of each of the saints," and who is descended from Muhammad on both his father's side (Hasani) and his mother's side (Hussaini).[8] From him

7. This is the report that God said to Muhammad, "If not for you I would not have created the cosmos"; this is another hadith qudsi that is preserved by many different hadith transmitters, as discussed in Schimmel, *Mystical Dimensions of Islam,* 215 and Schimmel, *And Muhammad is His Messenger: The Veneration of the Prophet in Islamic Piety* (Chapel Hill: University of North Carolina, 1985), 131–35.

8. Shaykh ʿAbd al-Qadir Jilani died in 1258 in Baghdad. He is known by many praise names like Mahbub-i Subhani (Beloved of God) and Piran Pir (Master of Masters) and Pir-i Dastagir (Master of the Helping Hand). He was a Sayyid who was descended from the Prophet Muhammad on his father's side through Imam Hasan and on his mother's side through Imam Hussain. From him all Qadiri Sufis trace their spiritual allegiance.

its teachings came through a succession of inspired guides to Shaykh Muhiy al-Din the Second.[9] From him initiation came directly to Maulana Shah, the greatest sage of his era and from him it came me who writes these lines.[10]

In that night of inspiration, I was also commanded to write this treatise to show plainly the way to reach God for those who search for guidance towards the truth. To distinguish it from the other books of this type, I consulted the Majestic Qur'an in order to give it a proper title according to divine inspiration. So I have named it *The Compass of Truth* (*Risala-i Haqq-Numa*). This is because when I consulted the Qur'an, I read this verse: "After we had destroyed the old generation, we gave the message to Moses that might be a guide and mercy for the people, that they might remember the truth."[11] This verse is perfectly suitable to express the meaning of this book, so it is called *The Compass of Truth.*

If you desire union, so your heart is a garden in flower
You must dedicate yourself to searching for your lover
Take this as your guide, like a compass pointing out Mecca
To show you God, only divine light itself has the power!

Khwahi keh dil-at ze wasl gardad gulshan
Khud ra tu bi-just-o-ju-yi dil-bar afgan
An qibla numa chu qibla mi-yaband
Daryab ze haqq numa-yi haqq ra roshan

So let those read this book who have not been ennobled by keeping the company of a perfect spiritual guide or have never

9. Makhdum ʿAbd al-Qadir Sani ("the second") died in 1533 in Uchh (now in Pakistan near Multan). He helped to spread the Qadiri Sufi order in Northern India.

10. Mawlana Shah was the Sufi guide of Dara Shikoh. He is usually called Mulla Shah or Muhammad Shah Badakhshi (died in 1661). He was buried next to his Sufi guide, the great Qadiri teacher of Lahore, Miyan Mir (died 1635). See Schimmel, *Empire of the Great Mughals: History, Art and Culture* (London: Reaktion Books, 2004), 135.

11. Surat al-Qisas 28:43.

met a perfect guide. Let them study it deeply and carefully, and put into practice its advice point by point. If they do so, there is hope that they might reach the goal and achieve an understanding of pure divine unity (*mashrab-i safi-yi tawhid*), for the furthest perfection of humanity lies in this mystical knowledge (*ʿirfan*). In these pages, they can find the inner meaning of all the books written by early and later mystics, which are too voluminous for them to read. By this, they might understand the essential meaning of all the great Sufi books such as *al-Futuhat al-Makkiya* and *Fusus al-Hikam* by Ibn ʿArabi, and commentaries on them like *Sawanih* (Inspirations from the World of Pure Spirits) by Ahmad Ghazali, *Lawaʾih* (Divine Gleams) by Mawlana Jami and *Lamaʿat* (Divine Flashes) by Fakhr al-Din ʿIraqi.[12]

> If for you the inner essence of the law is abstruse
> To really criticize Sufi texts you're far too obtuse
> Recognize one and no other in this world and the next
> This is the truth taught in the *Futuhat* and the *Fusus*

---

12. These books describe the oneness of being (*wahdat-i wujud*) in terms that combine Sufism and philosophy. Ibn Arabi's classic text, *Fusus al-Hikam,* has been translated into English as *Ibn Arabi: The Bezels of Wisdom,* trans. Ralph Austin (Mahwah, NJ: Paulist Press, 1980); the greatest Persian commentary upon it was by ʿAbd al-Rahman Jami, *Naqd al-Nusus fi sharh Naqsh al-Fusus,* alluded to in the poem in the phrase "criticize Sufi texts." Ibn Arabi's magnum opus, *al-Futuhat al-Makkiyya,* is analyzed cogently in James Morris, *The Reflective Heart: Discovering Spiritual Intelligence in Ibn ʿArabī's Meccan Illuminations* (Louisville: Fons Vitae, 2005); and also James Morris and William Chittick, *Ibn ʿArabī: The Meccan Revelations* (New York: Pir Press, 2002). Other famous and controversial Sufi texts on the oneness of being include *Sawanih* by Ahmad Ghazali, published as *Inspirations from the World of Pure Spirits,* trans. Nasrollah Pourjavady (New York: Methuen, 1986); and *Jami, Lawaih: Treatise on Sufism,* transl. E. H. Whinfield and Mirza Muhammad Kazvini (1906; reprinted London: Theosophical Publishing House, 1978); and *Lamaʿat* by Fakhr al-Din Iraqi, published as *Fakhruddin ʿIraqi: Divine Flashes,* transl. William Chittick and Peter Lamborn Wilson (Mahwah, NJ: Paulist Press, 1982).

Tu batin-i shar' gar na-dani bi-khusus
Darhum na-kuni nazar tu bar naqd-i nusus
Yek dan o ma-dan tu ghayr-i u dar do jahan
In ast haqiqat-i Futuhat o Fusus

All that is written in this book records exactly the methods of behaving and meditating, sitting and standing, exercising and practicing that were laid down by the Prophet Muhammad, may God bless him and his family. It contains not the slightest deviation from his example.

If a person who has reached God should happen to read this book, he will recognize how well I have shown the way to the divine threshold, and how wide I have opened the doors of renunciation and wisdom, so that worldly people may know plainly that the bounty of God has no fault or flaw. God draws anyone whom God wills towards the divine in whatever condition they may be! This is a fortune that not everyone can get. Rather, I have been specifically chosen for this good fortune.

In the days of my youth, I heard in a dream that a divine voice proclaimed four times, "God has provided you with that which no ruler on the face of the earth ever got!" On awaking, I interpreted this to mean that I shall receive mystical knowledge (*'irfan*), and I always expected the day when this illumination would come to me. In time, its effects began to show, and day by day the results of it became clearer. In those days, I was wracked by the pain of searching, but I had full faith in this community of Sufis. In those days, I wrote a book about the lives of the spiritual guides who belonged to this community in the past; in it I recorded their spiritual states and mystical stations, the dates of birth, the length of their lives, and the places of their burial, and I titled that book *Ship of the Saints* (*Safinat al-Awliya*). After that I was ennobled by having taken initiation, engaged in mystical practices and became knowledgeable about the stations of the Sufi way; at that time I composed a second book on the signs, behavior, stations and the miracles of my own spiritual guides, entitled *Deliverance of the Saints* (*Sakinat al-Awliya*).

It was at this time that God opened for my heart the doors of mystical knowledge and unity (*tawhid*), and bestowed upon me special disclosures of divine presence (*futuhat*) and outpourings of grace (*fayuzat*). Whatever has been written in this book has the quality that the Qur᾿an explains: "in it there is divine mercy and a reminder for those who believe."[13] In the way of the Qadiri order, the way explained in this book, there is no hardship or difficulty, contrary to the practices laid down in other orders.

> I see in it no exertion—it is grace given free as a breeze
> Kindness and love here is all, here all is pleasure and ease
>
> *Riyazat nist pesh-i ma hameh luft ast o bakhsha᾿ish*
> *Hameh mahr ast o dildari hameh ῾aysh ast o asa᾿ish*

Your spiritual guide ought to be such that he leads you to God without difficult practices and hardships, rather than one who causes you much pain and trouble in order to reach God. As Ibn ῾Ata said, "Your guide is one who shows you the way to your tranquility not one who leads you to your difficulty."[14] Likewise, Mawlana Rumi says:

> You were brought along this path to be welcomed
> You were not brought here merely to be punished
>
> *Ze chandin rah bi-mahmaniyat avurad*
> *Na-avurad-at bara-yi intiqam-i u*

O my friend, listen well! In the path of the Sufis, initiates do not call each other "disciple" but rather they call each other "friend" (*yar*). Even the blessed Prophet used to call his followers "friends" and "companions" (*ashab*)—among them

---

13. Surat al-῾Ankabut 29:51.

14. In Arabic, this saying by Ibn ῾Ata is: "*Shaykhu-ka man yadullu-ka ῾ala rahati-ka la man yadullu-ka ῾ala ta῾bi-ka.*"

the words "master" (*pir*) and "disciple" (*murid*) were not used. Therefore, whenever this book mentions the word "friend" you should understand it to mean a seeker of God (*talib*). Know that this book consists of four chapters and in each chapter describes one of the four worlds (*'alam*) or planes of existence.

Chapter 1: On the Phenomenal World

By the term "phenomenal world" (*'alam-i nasut*), we mean this world that is perceived through sensory experience. Some call it the visible world (*shahadat*) or simply the created world (*mulk*); others call it the world of waking consciousness (*bi-dar*) or the world-as-believed (*pindar*). It is in this world that ultimate being is most present, and in which delight and enjoyment is most perfect.

My friend, when the troubled soul searches for the true One in this phenomenal world, the first thing that he should do is to find some solitary quiet corner and sit there alone in meditation. He should hold in mind the image of the spiritual guide in whom he believes or the image of someone whom he loves deeply. He should imagine this person by closing the eyes and focusing concentration of the heart so that with the vision of the heart he sees the image of the guide or beloved.

My friend, in the opinion of this humble seeker, the heart can be said to exist in three places. The first place is within the chest towards the left side, and it is the physical organ of the heart, of flesh shaped like a pine cone (*dil-i sanubari*). This physical heart is possessed by all men as well as animals.

The flesh that is shaped like the human heart
Ask your butcher! Of every animal it is a part

an-che bi-surat dil-i insan bud
bar dar-i qassab farawan bud

This is true, but this is not what those who have mystical knowledge mean when they refer to the heart.

The second place wherein the heart is said to reside is the source of the mind (*umm al-dimagh*). It is called the spherical heart (*dil-i mudawwar*) and is sometimes called the heart that is pure of all qualities (*be-rang*). It has the special quality that when the seeker concentrates upon this spherical heart, no stray thought or temptation affects him, because no negative thought (*khatra*) can reach that place. The third place is in the very center of the seat of the body (*nishast-gah*), and this is called the lotus heart (*dil-i nilofari*).[15]

Now when one meditates as mentioned above, one concentrates at the place of the physical heart. The images that appear to the vision of one's heart constitute the imaginative world (*ʿalam-i-misal*). This imaginative world of thought-forms is the means to open into the spiritual world (*ʿalam-i malakut*). To make this opening clear, it is described as different from the spiritual world and is called the imaginative world; but in reality the imaginative world is part and parcel of the spiritual world.

My friend, when you devote yourself to holding in mind the image (of your spiritual guide or beloved) in the way described above, you will find that gradually the imagined form will increasingly correspond with that of which it is an image. As this correspondence increases, it will become an effective means of opening the spiritual world (*ʿalam-i malakut*). As the image becomes clear and definitive in your mind, then you will be blessed with an opening of the imaginative world. As you remain intensely engaged in this exercise, you will witness things that would otherwise be hidden from your perception.

15. The image of the heart as a lotus is very ancient in India. In his commentary on the *Yoga Sutra* of Patanjali. Vacaspati writes, "Painless lucidity means that which is devoid of pain. The state of lucidity is the light shining in the lotus of the heart. Let the mind be concentrated upon the lotus which is located between the chest and the abdomen. It has eight petals and is placed with its face downward. Its face has first to be turned upwards by the process of the expirative control of breath." Guy Beck, *Sonic Theology: Hinduism and Sacred Sound*, 89.

Chapter 2: On the Spiritual World

This is the spiritual world *('alam-i malakut)* which is also called the world of spirits (*arwah*) or of the unseen (*ghayb*); some also call it the subtle world (*latif*) or the world of dreaming (*khwab*). The phenomenal world is ephemeral, but this world, the spiritual world, which is the source of the phenomenal world, is in no way ephemeral but rather subsists eternally.

> What is sleeping? just a light death
> What is dying? merely a heavy sleep
>
> *Mi-dani khwab che-st? margi-st sabuk*
> *Mi-dani marg che-st? khwabi-st giran*

My friend, the imaginative world—as described in the preceding section—is the key to opening the spiritual world. When, after closing one's eyes, one sees in the imagination forms in one's vision, they should be understood as images intended for the spirit not for the body.

It is clear that a person's spirit (*ruh*) that appears in human form in the phenomenal world actually exists beyond the bodily form; its presence can be called into one's vision at any time. Everyone who sleeps and dreams—whether consciously or unaware—thereby circulates in the spiritual world. This happens by means of the spirit taking up a subtle body of utmost subtlety (*jasadi latif-i latafat*) that is the exact counterpart of the physical body, with eyes, ears, tongue and all the senses and powers of the body, but without external physical organs of flesh and blood. Through this subtle body the spirit is present in the spiritual world.

While roaming through the spiritual world, those whose hearts are refined and aware see beautiful and subtle forms, hear exquisite voices and partake of delight. But those whose hearts are burdened with materiality and distraction see ugly forms and hear horrifying sounds during these wanderings. Such people do not encounter anything but what exists in the phenomenal world, and they feel no pleasure and delight in these wanderings.

Therefore my friend, if you practice with diligence and perseverance the methods of meditation described below, the rust of your heart will be removed and the mirror of your heart will become clear and bright. Then reflected in your heart you will be able to see the forms of prophets, saints and angels. There you will meet also the image of your spiritual guide (*murshid*) who will lead you to the holy Prophet (may the blessings of God be upon him and his descendants), and the noble companions of the Prophet and the powerful saints. Whatever difficulties you might have, you can ask for their solutions from these images through the voice of your heart and the language of your spiritual state, and you will receive an apt reply from them. Thus the faith of your heart will increase in certitude, and you will feel absolute tranquility in this spiritual world.

If you see an image that appears to be the holy Prophet, know it for sure that this is really the Prophet (may the blessings of God be upon him and his descendants) because there is an authentic hadith in which he says, "He who has seen my image verily has seen me because tempting spirits cannot appear in my image." It is clear that this saying refers to seeing the Prophet in the spiritual world.

Owing to alienation from knowledge of the divine, human nature inclined to coarseness and became separated from its original refinement and subtlety. Therefore, this spiritual world serves to show the way for the human being to return to original refinement. This is so that the human beings may realize that their original nature is subtle but has become overpowered by coarse materiality.

This is because the human being consists of both spirit (*ruh*) and body (*badan*). If a person is more drawn to the body than to the spirit, then that person's spirit takes on the quality of the body and becomes more dense and obscure and coarse. But if, on the other hand, a person is more drawn to the spirit than to the body, then the body itself takes qualities of the spirit and it becomes more subtle, clear and light. As an illustration, the holy Prophet, that Leader of men, inclined more towards the spirit and exerted control over the body, such that his body itself had become extremely rarified and refined—so much so, that no fly ever landed on him and he did not cast any shadow on the ground. It was like air which is also refined; no fly can land on air, and it casts no shadow. Yet the spirit is even more subtle than air, such that nothing can obstruct its movement or prevent its activity. It is no wonder that the holy Prophet (may the blessings of God be upon him and his descendants) made his famous ascension to heaven (*mi'raj*) in his physical body. And it is similarly understandable that Jesus (may God's peace be upon him) is in the heavens in a physical body. For truly, "Our spirits are bodies and our bodies are our spirits."[16]

Therefore, my friend, when you proceed through this imaginative world (*'alam-i misal*) into the spiritual world, you will realize that you can see there human spirits both good and bad, and you will find that angels even appear like the human spirits. When you experience this, be diligent to keep your concentration focused. You must stay focused on that spiritual world of subtlety for it is the true and original world, and the imaginative world of thought-forms and images is merely its shadow. You must stay focused on it until it becomes thoroughly clear to you. Then you will be able to see whatever you desire to see in the spiritual world. And when you have fully acclimatized yourself to the subtle world, then you will be blessed with an opening (*fath*) into the spiritual world.

But always remember that the ultimate goal is not this! Do not let yourself remain entangled in this spiritual world, for

16. This saying in Arabic—*Arwahu-na ajsadu-na wa ajsadu-na arwahu-na*—is attributed to the Shi'i Imams and it is well loved by Sufis; see Seyyed Hossein Nasr, *Religion and the Order of Nature* (New York: Oxford University Press, 1996), 252.

you must find release from the engrossing whirlpool of this spiritual world. You should not content yourself with seeing its forms and images. You should not resign your heart to this world of appearances. You should never desire amazing disclosures (*kashf*) and miraculous powers (*karamat*) from it. Indeed, in this spiritual world there are wonderful powers of knowledge and ability, and with its help you can perform many miracles. For example, consider the following story.

Once a boil developed on the eyelid of that blessed spiritual guide Miyan Mir. It was very painful, and he suffered much because of it. A surgeon was called in. He was asked the best way to treat it, and he said, "The sty must be lanced." Just then Miyan Natha, one of the spiritually adept companions of Miyan Mir, interjected saying, "Wait for just a moment," and directed his concentration to the spiritual world (*ʿalam-i malakut*). There he saw a person and asked him, "What might be the remedy for the boil which had grown on the eyelid of Miyan Mir?" That spiritual being replied, "Grind cucumber seeds into a poultice and apply this to the boil." Miyan Natha opened his eyes and said, "Do not cut open this boil on the eyelid of Miyan Mir, but rather apply a poultice of cucumber seed on it." A paste of ground cucumber seed was made and rubbed on the sty, and it immediately relieved the problem. One present there asked Miyan Mir, "Does Miyan Natha have expert knowledge in eye diseases?" He replied, "He does not! Rather, in the spiritual world there are remedies for any problem. Miyan Natha simply directed his concentration (*tawajjuh*) to the spiritual realm, and from there he was told this remedy. Whatever is told in the spiritual world to one with a saintly heart (*sahib-dil*), without a doubt that will come to pass." The person inquired again, "Do you not have the ability to get the remedy from the spiritual world yourself, that Miyan Natha had to find the cure for you?" Miyan Mir answered, "I have gone beyond the spiritual world, and to turn my concentration to that realm would be below my station."

So it is, O friend, that many Sufis have gotten distracted by performing miracles in bargaining with the spiritual realm and have thereby missed the essential goal. Do not think that one should never enter this spiritual world! No, rather one should not get too comfortable there, for the spiritual realm is a station that the saints of God must pass through and transcend. Every spiritual seeker must pass through that place, but should never allow one's attention to get deflected into that place. If one tarried there, the path becomes forked into a hundred paths in which he will be lost.

In the way of the Sufis, conquering the spiritual world is a great conquest (*fath-i ʿuzma*) for any mystic. This was the method of Shaykh ʿAbd al-Qadir Jilani.[17] It is related by Shaykh ʿUmar Abu Jandiqi that, "Once I went to see Shaykh ʿAbd al-Qadir, the leader of all sages. He put a cap on my head, and its pleasant and cool sensation pervaded my mind, and from my mind it penetrated into my heart. The spiritual world was revealed to me, and I heard the whole universe and all that existed in it glorifying God in different melodies and varied ways of declaring holy, holy, holy. It almost reached the point that my reason was overwhelmed, but the Shaykh put a piece of cotton into my ears and thereby preserved my intellect."

My friend, when this spiritual world and realm of images becomes opened for you and conquest of it is granted, you must practice for some time the exercises (*ashghal*) of this Sufi path, so that your heart will be purified and illuminated. In this way, you must clear away the rust that has settled on the mirror of your heart, so that you may witness in it the beloved's beauty. The heart is said to be the divine throne of the merciful One (*ʿarsh-i rahman*). The meaning of this saying is that the spiritual reality of the divine essence (*haqiqat-i zat*) is cast into the human heart, and by focusing one's concentration there,

---

17. Throughout this text, ʿAbd al-Qadir Jilani is usually referred to by his honorific title *Hazrat Ghawth al-Saqalain* or "His Highness the Succor of Both Worlds."

the senses that are dispersed in anxious confusion become gathered into unity.

The great spiritual guide Miyan Mir used to tell his disciple, "You should recite the name of God (Allah) without moving the tongue, and gradually it will be recited by the heart. By constantly repeating this blessed name of God in the way described above, one will be granted a spiritual state (*hal*) in which one's heart remains awake and aware even when one is sleeping." My friend, this name—Allah—is the greatest name. It is universal and is common to both those who believe in Islam and who do not. In it are gathered into unity all the diverse names. There is nothing existing in the universe that is outside this name. This name is known as "the greatest name" (*ism-i aʿzam*), and this is because it possesses three attributes: creation, preservation and destruction. The whole creation and every atom of matter is integrally related to these three attributes, but no one is aware of this. And nobody knows the secret meaning of the greatest name except some of the great realized spiritual masters who are extremely rare.

The method of spiritual practice which has been adopted by this lowly seeker is the suspension of breath (*habs-i nafas*). I have found this method to be the best and choicest method, without which success cannot be obtained. So everyone ought to practice this method of suspending the breath. Let it be done in this way. Sit in a secluded spot in the posture in which the holy Prophet—may God grant him blessings and peace—used to sit (on one's knees as if for prayer), but do not place the hands upon the knees. Rather, place each elbow on the knees and reach up with the hands, and with the thumb close the hole of each ear so that no air may pass out of them. With the index fingers shut both eyes in such a way that the upper eyelid may remain firmly pressed against the lower eyelid, but without the fingers pressing on the eyeballs. Place the ring finger and pinkie of each hand on the upper and lower lips, so as to close the mouth and not permit breath to pass through it. Place the two middle fingers on the sides of the nose, the right middle finger on the right nostril, and the left middle finger on the left nostril.

Having assumed this posture, first firmly close the right nostril with the right middle finger, so that air may not come through it. Leaving open the left nostril, breathe in slowly through the left nostril while saying "No god" (*la ilaha*) through that breath; while inhaling you draw the breath up above the mind and then bring it down to the heart. After this, also close firmly the left nostril with the left middle finger, and thus suspend the breath within the body. This is called "suspension of breath " (*habs-i nafas*). Keep the breath suspended as long as you can easily do so without feeling suffocation. As you continue this practice, keep increasing slowly, by increments, the duration of suspending the breath. Then you should release the breath, opening the right nostril by removing the middle finger from it. As you exhale slowly and gently, you should say "but God" (*illa 'llah*) through the breath. If you exhale the breath quickly or forcefully, it will be injurious to you. Then you repeat this process (drawing in the breath through the left nostril, keeping both nostrils closed for some time, and releasing the breath through the right nostril).

Some who practice this method of meditation have carried this to such a extent that they pass the entire day of twelve hours by drawing in only four breaths. But my own spiritual guide, Mullah Shah (may God grant him peace and sustain his life) carried the practice to the point that he would, after making his night-time prayer (*namaz-i isha*), draw in a breath and keep it suspended, not releasing it until the time for the dawn prayer; he would keep a single breath suspended within him for the whole night, whether it was a long night of winter or a short night of summer. For fifteen years, he spent his nights in this way. Through the effect of this practice, he obtained a great conquest (*fath-i 'uzma*) and the doors of spiritual fortune were opened to him.

One of the benefits of this practice is that it eliminates the need for sleep. Thus it is now thirty years that Mullah Shah has not slept. This noble practice removes the rust from the mirror of the heart and purifies the defilements of the body. I have learned this practice, through a series of realized and actualized masters, from Shaykh ʿAbd al-Qadir Jilani (may the peace of the God be with him). He himself gave this practice a name and established its method, and he called it "engaged and conquered" (*avurd o burd*). Our great Qadiri master, Miyan Mir, made a small addition to the above method. He taught that during the period when the breath was kept suspended, the practitioner should repeat the words "No god" (*la ilaha*) with the voice of the physical organ of the heart (*dil-i sanubari*). While suspending the breath, the mind should not remain idle because an idle mind gives opportunity for negative thoughts. But when one concentrates on reciting "but God" (*illa ʾllah*), all tempting thoughts are removed and one's mind is restrained from focusing on any other object. Miyan Mir called this method of removing tempting thoughts while doing suspension of breath "struck and conquered" (*zad o burd*), because anyone who has struck the noble name of God on the target of his heart has scored the goal.[18]

My friend, on this spiritual path there are many kinds of distracting and tempting thoughts, so Miyan Mir has established several methods of averting them so that these thoughts have no way of access to the seeker's heart. The technique mentioned above (reciting "No god but God" during the duration of suspending the breath) is one among these methods. Another method is useful for anyone who suffers much from tempting thoughts while meditating. Concentrating on the physical organ of the heart (*dil-i sanubari*) can give rise to many such thoughts because the physical heart is the locus of

18. Here Dara Shikoh uses images from polo (striking the ball against the target to score a goal and win the challenge) to describe mystical practices. Polo was a Central Asian sport that was brought to India with the Afghans and Turks. For an earlier example of this imagery, see Arifi, *The Ball and the Polo Stick or The Book of Ecstasy*, transl. Wheeler Thackston and Hossein Ziai (Bibliotheca Iranica: Intellectual Traditions Series, No.3).

temptations and distractions; therefore, a person in this condition should focus concentration instead on the spherical heart (*dil-i mudawwar*) and not on the physical organ that is shaped like a pine cone. Because the spherical heart is pure of all qualities (*be-rang*), it provides no way of access for tempting thoughts, and distractions which cannot lodge there. Another method of removing tempting thoughts is to consider them as not separate from yourself and not something other than you.

My friend, when you have engaged for some time in this noble practice of suspending the breath in the method described above, you will feel a wondrous heat, a strange buoyancy, a great longing, and a subtle illumination in your heart that pervades your entire being. This will totally banish the coarse qualities of distraction and negligence (*ghaflat*) which will completely vanish. Then you will feel a great spiritual delight (*zauq*) and indescribable ecstasy (*wajd*). The sweet delight of this practice, once tasted, will keep you from all idleness and indigence.

But this practice has its limitations: it cannot be done at any time because a secluded place is a necessary condition for it. Therefore, so long as you are in a secluded place, you can remain engaged in this noble practice. But when you are traveling or keeping the company of others, the first practice which was described above is more appropriate (namely, reciting the name of God silently in each breath), because it can be done at all times and places.

My friend, when you sit to practice suspending the breath, it is necessary that you persistently focus your concentration on your heart. This is because during this practice, voices will emerge from within you, just as Mawlana Rumi has described in his poem:

> On his lips is a lock but in his heart are secrets
> silence on the lips yet a heart full of voices
>
> *bar labb-ash qafl ast o dar dil-ash razeh*
> *labb-i khamosh o dil pur az avazeh*

This voice sometimes comes with a sound like a big cauldron boiling. Sometimes it comes like the buzzing sound heard in the nest of bees. It is to this internal sound that one of the early Sufi masters has alluded:

Constant as the whispering hum of ants
I listen for divine speech in my ear
God is like a sun lighting the universe
But lowly ones ask, "The divine is where?"

sukhan-ha bin keh az moran numayad
chu andar gosh-i ma goyad kalam u
hameh ʿalam girifteh aftabi
zehi gori keh mi-goyad kudam u

Be careful, my friend, not to think that this sound is merely a voice within you. No, the whole universe is pervaded by this voice within each thing and beyond each thing.

Remove the cotton of conceit from your ears
Partake of the sound of the overpowering One
A call eternally coming from the one true being
Why wait to hear it on the day of judgment?

Bar avur panbeh-yi pindar-at az gosh
nada-yi vahid al-qahhar bi-nosh
nada mi-ayad az haqq bar davamat
chera gashti tu mawquf-i qiyamat

The true nature of this sound will become apparent to you in a moment when this text describes the practice called "The Prime Recitation" (*sultan al-azkar*). This is the essential teaching of the Qadiri Sufi masters and is rare and precious these days. It has come down with authentic proof—both external and internal—from the blessed Prophet to ʿAbd al-Qadir Jilani, and from him to the great teacher Miyan Mir. This practice of hearing the divine sound is called in the path of the Sufis "The Dominating Power of Recitation" (*sultan al-azkar*). [19]

My friend, all sounds are of three kinds. The first kind is sound that is emitted when two objects strike against each other, like when the palms of the hands strike against each other and we hear the clap. But the motion of one hand alone cannot produce this external sound. This kind of sound is called "phenomenal" (*muhdath*) and "compound" (*murakkab*).

The second kind of sound is that which is produced without the contact of two dense bodies, or without the utterance of speech which is compounded from the mixing of the elements of heat and air within the human body.[20] This kind of sound is called "essential" (*basit*) and subtle (*latif*).

The third kind is the sound which is boundless and is eternal without any cause or means. This sound is fixed to one tone which neither increases nor decreases; it admits to no change and emits with no friction. Although the whole world is full of this primeval sound, yet none except the spiritually awakened know of it. This sound existed from before the creation of the existing things, exists even now, and will always exist. This sound is called "infinite" (*be-hadd*) and "absolute" (*mutlaq*).

There is no practice better than that of hearing this sound. This is because every other practice depends upon the will of the practitioner; if he for a moment stops it, the practice ceases. But not so this practice! It does not depend upon the will of the practitioner. It is present and available without ceasing and without interruption at all times.

From many authentic reports collected in the six authentic hadith collections, we learn that our Prophet (may the blessing

19. In *Kashkul-i Kalimi* this is called *Sultan al-Zikr,* but the meaning is the same; both are translated in English as "The Prime Recitation" to avoid confusion.

20. The idea that speech is the result of the mixing elemental heat (fire *atish*) and air (wind *bad*) is congruent with the ancient Indic idea, preserved in Hinduism, that *vac* or sacred speech arises from the mixing of fire and air.

and peace of God be on him) was devoted to this practice, both before the start of his mission as a prophet and after. But the religious scholars do not know the secret of its meaning and have not consequently followed the Prophet in this practice.

A story is related by Khadija (the Prophet's wife) that the Prophet, before he became a prophet, used to carry provisions with him and go stay in a cave. This was the cave of Hira, which is a famous and well-known place in the mountains outside of Mecca. He used to remain there for days together absorbed in this practice. There he used to practice this hearing of sound, which resulted in his being able to see the form of Gabriel before him. In this way, divine revelation began for that leader of humankind. That was start of it all, and all that happened after it, happened because of it.

My friend, when you want to begin this practice "The Prime Recitation" (*sultan al-azkar*), and obtain this noble practice, you should do as follows. You must go either by day or by night to some deserted place which is free from the distractions of human interaction, or to a secluded and silent room. Sit there and direct your attention to your ears. Concentrate as hard and as long as you can until a very subtle sound manifests. Hearing this sound, it will gradually grow more powerful and overwhelming, so much so that will seem to come from all sides of you and there will be no place or no time when this sound will not manifest. This sound, which takes you away and beyond yourself, is a drop from the ocean of eternal resonance. So you can guess at its vastness.

> Sit in a corner with your own ear, then speak and hear
> The world is entirely full of his silent speaking voice
>
> *tu bi-gosh-i khwesh gushe bi-nah o bi-gu o bi-shanu*
> *keh jahan pur ast yek-sar ze sada-yi be-nava-esh*

It is said that Plato once said to Moses (may peace be upon him), "Are you the son of a menstruating woman, that you claim, 'My God speaks to me,' when the fact is that God is transcendent above place and time?" Moses replied, "Yes, I do claim that God talks to me, because from every side I hear a voice which is transcendent beyond beginning or end and is not compounded of syllables." When Plato heard this, he believed in Moses and acknowledged that he was a messenger of God.

Once people asked our Prophet (Muhammad) how revelation came to him. He replied, "I hear a sound sometimes like the sound of a boiling cauldron, and sometimes like the buzzing of honey bees, and sometimes in image of an angel in human form who speaks with me, and sometimes I hear a sound like resounding bells." The poet Hafiz alluded to this sound in his verse:

No one knows where the beloved resides
One gets only the sound of a bell from there

kas nadan-ast keh manzil-i dildar kuja-st
in qadar hast keh bang-i jarasi mi-ayad

Mawlana ʿAbd al-Rahman Jami has also described this sound when he writes:

To my beloved's caravan, I know, I can never draw near
It is enough that the peal of its bell always reaches my ear

dar qafilah keh u-st danam na-rasam
in bas keh rasad bi-gosh bang-i jaras-am

Miyan Mir used to explain that sometimes when the Prophet used to ride his camel, he would listen so intently to this eternal sound that he would be overwhelmed. At such times, he became so laden with power that his camel's knees would buckle under his weight, and it would sit down on the ground.[21]

21. Caravans were led by a camel with a bell around its neck, whose constant pealing would lead on the other camels and all followers.

My friend, the above description of how our Prophet received revelation is well known from reports that are preserved in the six canonical hadith collections. These hadith reports truly allude to hearkening to this primal sound (*sultan al-azkar*). Meditating by listening for this primordial sound, in the case of the prophets, allowed them to receive revealed scripture and divine commands. In contrast, in the case of saints (*awliya*), by meditating on this sound—without words, without source and without interruption—they find an immense power of will (*jam'iyat*), spiritual delight (*lazzat*), rapture (*wajd*), and ecstasy (*zauq*). So powerful is this experience that it makes them leave aside all other spiritual exercises and experiences in favor of the rapturous bliss of this meditation. Thus they dive deep into the ocean of this sound, and leave not a trace of their name and existence behind.[22]

Miyan Mir taught that 'Abd al-Qadir Jilani used to say, "Our Prophet was in the cave of Hira for six years engaged in this meditation on the primordial sound called "The Prime Recitation" (*sultan al-azkar*). I myself have spent twelve years in that same cave practicing this meditation, and through it I received many amazing spiritual disclosures."[23] Miyan Mir would comment, "I am bewildered by those pilgrims who undergo so much trouble and travel so far to Mecca to perform the Hajj rituals around the Ka'ba, yet do not go visit this holy cave to receive any blessing from that sacred place!"

---

22. The Maithri Upanishad describes this practice by stating, "By causing the tip of the tongue to turn back against the palate and by binding the senses, one may, as greatness, perceive greatness. Thence he goes to selflessness… By closing the ears with the thumbs they hear the sound of the space within the heart. Of it there is this sevenfold comparison: like rivers, a bell, a brazen vessel, a wheel, the croaking of frogs, rain, as when one speaks in a sheltered place." Beck, *Sonic Theology*, 46.

23. "Disclosure" in Persian is *kasha'ish*, which has the same meaning as *futuh* in Arabic. Abd al-Qadir Jilani wrote a book entitled *Futuh al-Ghayb* that is published as *Revelations of the Unseen: A Collection of Seventy-Eight Discourses by Shaykh Abd al-Qadir Jilani*, trans. Mukhtar Holland (n.p.: al-Baz Publishing, 1992).

Miyan Mir had such regard for this noble practice, my friend, that he did not mention it to most of his disciples and companions. When he did mention it to some of them, he usually couched his explanation in allusions and hints. In the case of my guide, Mulla Shah (Hazrat Akhund), it took him a whole year to realize the true nature of this meditation practice. Mulla Shah also explained this to me through allusions, and I realized it in six months. I in turn have taught this practice to others, and they have realized it very quickly, in only three or four days! The reason for this is that my spiritual guide and his guide used to speak of it by allusion and parable, while I have explained it clearly without veiling it at all.

When this sound manifests to your hearing, my friend, you must observe it keenly. You must try your hardest to preserve your ability to listen for it, until you can master it, so that just as you heard it in the silence of the wilderness or a closed room, you will also hear it in the noisy marketplace amid throngs of people. When you perfect this subtle and noble practice, this primordial sound will overpower the sounds of drums, even kettledrums or the loudest sounds which instruments can generate. And why should it not overpower them all, when it is the original source of them all, and every other sound manifests through it. Many disciples whom Miyan Mir had engaged in this practice used to go and sit in the marketplace amid the hustle and bustle, to test whether the sound heard in this noble meditation does indeed overpower all other sounds or not.

Congratulations and blessings, my friend, if you become capable of this practice called "The Prime Recitation" (*sultan al-azkar*). For then the subtle world becomes apparent to you, and also an absolute being that is constant and eternal. If you perform this subtle practice, it will cause you to become more subtle in your very being, and plunge you into the ocean of subtlety and absolute being, free of conditions and qualities (*itlaq be-rang*). Then from within your heart will surge up the ocean of reality, which is the fountainhead of your being. Then you will know for yourself that every sound and voice that exists in this universe has come into existence through this primordial sound. In the same way, you know that all that exists with form and color has taken on form and color through absolute being which is formless and without color. Just as that absolute being is an unlimited immensity, so also the form and color that arise from it are also unlimited. Similarly, the sound of absolute being is of an unlimited immensity. No other thing remains before it with form and color, and no other sound remains in its presence.

Chapter 3: The Realm of Divine Might

The realm of divine might (*ʿalam-i jabarut*) is also called the causal realm (*ʿalam-i lazim*) or the realm of singularity and empowerment (*ahadiyat o tamkin*). It is also called the formless realm (*be-naqsh*). Some Sufis call this the "realm of names and attributes" (*asma o sifat*), but they err in this. Many Sufis have realized this world of divine might and have therefore not understood it properly. If the "realm of names and attributes" exists as a world, then it must be considered as part of the spiritual realm. Or if it manifests in sensory perception, then it must be included in the human realm (*ʿalam-i nasut*). In either case, it is not correct to consider the "names and attributes" to be the same as the realm of divine might.

Only the great Sufi teacher ʿAbd al-Rahman Junaid has accurately described this realm. He says, "Being a Sufi means that you remain without grief, for even a moment." Shaykh al-Islam has asked, "Do you know what is the meaning of being without grief? It means finding without searching and seeing without looking, because seeing through the eyes is imperfect and weak."

Therefore, the realm of divine might is defined as a state of being in which one sees nothing that exists in the human realm or the spiritual realm. To such a person comes a state of oblivion (*mahwiyat*) when he experiences tranquility upon tranquility, and concentration within concentration (*jam'iyat*). In this state, he does not care whether he is aware or ignorant of his own being in the human realm or the spiritual realm, and neither he does not care about being in the realm of divine might! Imagine a person who is heedless to his surroundings because he is in deep sleep, and is therefore unaware of the human realm and looks for nothing in the spiritual realm. He would say, "I was sleeping tranquilly and peacefully and I saw nothing in my sleep." Being in the realm of divine might is like this: one is not conscious of any phenomenon in the human realm and is not aware of any event in the spiritual realm, yet knows bliss and joy. One understands it if one can sit for even a moment free of grief and pain, to which Abu'l-Qasim Junaid had alluded.

One is experiencing the realm of divine might when one, in a waking state, is aware of no sensory forms or spiritual experiences, similar to one in a deep and blissful sleep. But there is a huge difference between a person who experiences this in a waking state and who experiences it only in sleep! The later experiences it without willing to experience it. But the former wills to experience it whether in a waking state or in sleep, and chooses to go into the realm of divine might.

This is the posture for sitting when one wants to enter the realm of divine might. One should sit with tranquility and at ease. All the limbs of the body should be perfectly relaxed and free from any motion. Both the eyes should be closed. The right hand should rest overtop of the left. Then make the heart empty of all forms whether sensory or spiritual. No form should arise before one's outer sight or inner vision. Thus when one can sit without any thought or image crossing one's mind, one has found the realm of divine might. Only a person whom God wills to know this will realize the secret meaning of being in this realm.

Chapter 4: The Divine Realm

The divine realm (*ʿalam-i lahut*) is sometimes also called the realm of he-is-he (*huwiyat*) or the realm of essence (*zat*), or the realm of purity (*be-rang*) or realm of absolute being (*itlaq*), or the realm of suchness (*bahs*). This realm is the origin and source for the human realm, the spiritual realm and the realm of divine might. It encompasses all these other realms. In relation to it, these realms are like the body and the divine realm is like the soul. They all derive from it and are animated by it and depend upon it and revert to it. Yet in and of itself, it is independent and unchanging in its essence. As the Qurʾan says, "God is the first and the last, the apparent and the hidden, and God is the knower of all things."[24] This divine realm encompasses and surpasses all the other realms just like the ocean encompasses the waves that it contains, or like the sun surpasses the dust motes that it illumines, or just as meaning transcends the words through which it manifests.

My friend, turn all your faculties towards comprehending this divine realm when it begins to manifest to you, for from it springs all eternal bliss of witnessing divine unity (*tawhid*) and all never-ending fortune realizing the truth (*tahqiq*).

Chapter 5: The Divine Truth (Huwiyat)

You should realize that "All is he" (*hamah u-ast*). Then ask who are you? You will be forced to admit that your very self is indeed the divine essence and can be nothing else! Then you will be free of the illusionary bonds of "I and you." This is the truth of divine unity (*haqiqat-i tawhid*) and the self-disclosure of the essence (*tajalli-i zati*) "in their selves if only you would see."[25] In order to comprehend the divine essence you must observe your own self. In this way, vain imagining (*wahm*) and whispered temptation (*waswasa*) should not find any way to inhabit

24. Sural al-Hadid 57:3.
25. Surat al-Fusilat 41:53. The whole verse reads "We will show them our signs on the horizons and in their selves if only you would see."

your heart such that you think existing things veil the essence from your comprehension.

Can your seeing ice obscure the fact that the ice is water
Even when the form of a bubble is trapped in the ice?
God is an ocean of reality on which floats this world
As ice floats on water, yet water is what makes up ice

har giz na kunad ab hijab andar yakh
ba-an-keh kunad naqsh hubab andar yakh
haqq bahr-i haqiqat ast o kawnain dar-u
chun yakh bi-miyan-i ab o ab andar yakh

If any distracting thought comes to you, just consider it also to be one with the divine essence. Then just as the divine essence is perfect, its perfection will come to dominate that distracting thought and it will no long be a distraction. When your state reaches perfection in this way, wherever you look you will see yourself and whatever place you search for you will find yourself.

Beware of thinking that the divine essence is wholly characterized by transcendence (*tanazzuh*) and purity and absence of all qualities, lest you might remain untouched by the bliss of the divine's being related by similarity to existing things (*tashbih*). Likewise beware of thinking that the divine essence is characterized solely by similarity and resemblance, lest you miss out of the great gift of recognizing the divine's incomparable difference from all that exists (*tanzih*). Enough! Purity and impurity, transcendence and immanence, all are manifest and take their existence from this divine essence. If you imagine that a single mote of dust is separate from the divine essence then you have lost the blessing of witnessing divine unity (*tawhid*) and mystical comprehension (*ʿirfan*).

My friend, when the ocean of divine reality stirs, then waves and forms appear upon its surface. It generates a hundred thousand bubbles and swirls that are the innumerable heavens and earths that emerge in this cosmos. All this multiplicity emerges from that singular ocean and can never be separate from it! If you wanted to separate a wave or a pattern from the surface of the ocean, could you ever achieve this? Never. Although these things are separate in name and designation, they are united in essence and in ultimate reality they are one.

Shall I tell you of unity, so no misgiving persists?
Apart from God there is nothing that really exists
Those things that you see and think separate
In essence all is one, but each of a name consists

Tawhid bi-goyam, ar bi-fahmi bada
mawjud na-bud heech gah ghayr khuda
An-ha keh tu mi-beeni o mi-dani ghayr
dar zat hamah yeki-st o dar nam juda

Chapter 6: Recognizing Reality

Consider the reality of water. When water is not bound, it is free of color and has no fixed form. But when water is bound in a solid, it assumes various forms such as ice or snow or hail. Observe closely and decide for yourself whether or not the ice, snow and hail consist of the same essential water which is itself colorless and formless. When ice, snow and hail become melted, they all become resolved into water—then do you call it water or something else? All who recognize reality and who have eyes to see the truth will readily recognize the essential nature of water despite the various forms and appearance that it can adopt under different conditions.

The ocean of existence is just the essence so generous
like patterns on the water are spirits and soul numerous
it is a singular sea which is stirred into motion diverse
here a drop, there a wave, everywhere bubbles tenuous

darya-st wujud sirf zat-i wahhab
arvah o nufus ham-chu naqsh andar ab
bahri-st keh mauj bi-zanad andar khud
gah qatrah gah ast mauj gahi-st hubab

Those who are ignorant are bound up in seeing superficial appearance, phenomenal condition and apparent difference. This is the difference between the ignorant and the sages. Mystical knowledge (*ʿirfan*) is nothing but this: that you recognize your own real nature. Then you will realize that you are nothing but the divine essence, since all are one (*hame u-st*). It is impossible that anything exists other than God.

There are many metaphors to depict this reality. For example, on a page are depicted a picture, words and the meaning; all appear through the mediation of ink and appear to be different, yet all are in reality one. Or for example, the root, leaf, branch and fruit of a tree appear to be different, but all are in reality from the singular seed. The diversity and multiplicity of appearances do not negate the essential unity from which it all arises.

Essential unity against all duality raves
If you're blind, find a cure which saves
From one come many, yet it is still one
The ocean is never separate from waves

kardah az yiganigi duʾi ra taraj
bayad keh kuni kaj-i khud ra tu ʿilaj
vahid mutakassar na-shavad az iʿdad
darya mutajazzi na-shavad az amvaj

For the sake of brevity, this text contents itself with only the illustrations given above.

My friend, the absolute essence—the sun of ultimate reality and height of unqualified divinity—is described in the saying "I was a hidden treasure." When that essence manifests in intimacy with you, it makes clear the saying "I loved to be known."[26] Then the essence discards the veil of concealment, and the perfection of the essence becomes limited in a form for the sake of taking delight in union and beholding itself in a gaze of love. Now if you seek union with absolute being (*mutlaq*), you cannot find it except in a form that is limited (*muqayyad*). Likewise, if you seek that hidden treasure in a limited form, you cannot find it except in the absolute.

The absolute is always in the limited, and the limited is always with the absolute. It is truth that the limited form is not a veil obscuring absolute being. Existing beings do not exist independently from the absolute being. No! Rather, whatever you lay hands upon is a being that manifests the very essence of absolute divine being without any obscuring concealment. Whatever you may see is a disclosure of the beauty of absolute being without any obscuring veil.

There is nothing in this universe that is other than you
Whatever comes before you is just you confronting you

nist biganah kas darin ʿalam
dast bar har cheh mi-nahi khud pish

To the same effect is the following quatrain:

I'll tell you advice, for good thought it is fodder
If you're a man never leave the path to God's presence
Its manifestations can never veil the divine essence
Do ripples on water keep one from touching the water?

goyam sukhani ze ru-yi tahqiq o savab
gar mard rahi qabul kun ruʾi ma-tab
har giz na-bud sifat o zat hijab
ki naqsh bar ab maniʿ ast u mass-i ab

---

26. This is a saying or hadith qudsi which reports that God said, "I was a hidden treasure and I loved to be known, so I created the cosmos that I might be known"; see Schimmel, *Mystical Dimensions of Islam*, 189.

This leads to the last and greatest method of meditation, my friend, in this noble Sufi way. That is to sit grasping one's own true nature, such that, in spite of all your limitations, consider yourself as the very absolute being and only existence. In this state, whatever comes to your sight as other than yourself you should recognize as identical to your self. In this way one extirpates the very root of duality and discards the veils of alienation and separation. One sees everything as partaking of one essence, and realizes the bliss of self merging with self, as alluded to in this verse:

My beloved Laila, from me or Majnun can never
    be separate
From the circle of its rays of light, a candle can never
    be separate

Yar-i laila-vash-i man ghayr-i man o majnun nist
Shama ʿaz daʾira-yi partau-yi khud birun nist

And on this very subject a great Sufi once alluded, saying:

From my own bosom I discover each moment
    the aroma of him I love
So I always draw my own self to my bosom
    in a constant embrace

Az kinar-i khwesh mi-yabam damadam bu-yi yar
ze an hamin giram hamesha khweshtan ra dar kinar

My friend, those who have firmly realized this intimate relation (*nisbat*) are ennobled by true knowledge of the real self which is greatest elixir [that endows eternal life] and the rarest red sulfur [which brings everlasting happiness]. They obtain release from wandering in the wilderness of negligence and ignorance, and gain liberation from the anxiety of searching and craving, and are free from the doubts and temptations of dispute.

A drop is just a drop as long as it believes it is separate
from the sea
A man is bound by his limited self until he knows that
God is he

qatra qatra ast ta na pindarad keh az darya juda-st
banda band-i khweshtan ra ta na-mi-danad khuda-st

A similar idea is expressed in this quatrain:

Hey you, who are lost searching for divinity
You're other than God? You're God in reality!
In your foolish searching you are just like
A drop in the depths that searches for the sea

Ay an-keh khuda'i ra bi-ju'i har ja
tu 'ain-i khuda'i na juda'i bi-khuda
in justan-i tu hamin bi-an mi-manad
qatrah bi-miyan-i ab o juyad darya

When you have reached this highest level, then over you arises the sun of spiritual reality and essential unity. Then are lifted from you all the traces of delusion and selfish conceit. At this point, the veil of darkness is removed from you.

As long as a veil remains between you and your love
You long for the beauty and perfection of his face
Yet your frame of vision is the veil you long to remove
Abandon the frame, so no dust of dualism leaves a trace

har chand niqab dar miyan darad yar
ru-yash khush o khub mi-numayad besyar
chun 'ainak-i tu bud niqab-i rukh-i yar
'ainak na kunad bi pish chashm-i tu ghubar

At this level, all are unified as one: the meditation, the one meditating, and the object of meditation (*zikr o zakir o mazkur*). The author of the book *Divine Flashes* (*Lama'at* by Fakhr al-Din 'Iraqi) describes this station beautifully:

In this place beloved, love and lover are all one not three
If there is no scope for union, how can there separation be?

maʿshuq o ʿishq o ʿashiq har seh yeki-st in-ja
chun vasl dar na-gunjad hijran cheh kar darad

When a spiritual guide has led the sincere seeker to this level and allowed him to understand this subtle principle, then the guide dedicates him to God and leaves off teaching him any further. There is no more scope for teaching, because it is not right for one to try to teach God.

My friend when you come to know this essential principle and thereby realize what is the real meaning of distance and alienation from the beloved, then may you always be happy.

In separation from you I suffered anxiety
From union with you I lost my life and piety
What bliss it is that enraptures my being
Now my body and soul enjoy tranquility

dar hijr-tu budeh anduh azar-am
az vasl-i tu raft hasti o pindar-am
shadi amad nasib-i jan-am gardid
aknun tan o jan khud bi-rahat daram

At that point, your own being has become one with universal being. Therefore, from your heart is lifted sorrow, anxiety, delusion, duality and alienation. Fearing punishment and coveting reward are also gone, for your path is before you that leads to eternal liberation (*najat*). So now do whatever you desire, and live in whatever way you like.

Chose to get wisdom, my friend! Riches and power defer
If wisdom you have, then you'll get whatever else you chose

Badshahi ra guzar ay dost agahi guzin
chun agahi rasidi har-che mi-khwahi guzin

This verse of the Qur'an was also revealed to describe these spiritual masters: "No fear is upon them and they do not grieve."[27] And the good tidings of "tranquility descended into their heart" also refers to them and their spiritual state.[28]

My friend, there are many verses of the Qur'an, many reports from the Prophet, and many sayings of pious spiritual masters from earlier times that prove this point. If you long to discover the proof of this, know that you can witness the sun of truth in every speck of dust that is visible. When your spiritual relationship (*nisbat*) becomes complete and perfect, then not a mote of delusion or doubt will remain in your whole being. Then from within your own self, by its own volition, there will emerge a delight and bliss of realization (*tahqiq*). From witnessing the essential unity, your partial and individuated existence will become universal and holistic, like a drop becomes the ocean, like a dust particle glows in the sun, like from non-existence emerges pure being!

The Compass of Truth is done—here it will cease
In the year one-thousand and fifty-six I've said my piece
It comes not from a Qadiri but from the powerful One[29]
So understand what I've said and upon you be peace

In risalah-yi haqq-numa bashad tamam
dar hazar o panjah o shash shud tamam
hast az qadir madan az qadiri
an-cheh ma guftim fa-afham wa salam

This book is completed.

---

27. Surat Yunus 10:62. The whole verse reads, "For surely the friends of God there is no fear upon them and they do not grieve."
28. Surat al-Fath 48:4. The whole verse reads, "God it is who made tranquility descended into the hearts of the believers that they might increase in faith."
29. This poem concludes the book, gives its title, records the date of its composition, and specifies that the writer belongs to the Qadiri Sufi order. Yet he asserts that the book is not by a mere Qadiri who is a follower of Shaykh 'Abd al-Qadir, rather is by God the powerful One (*qadir*).

Treatise on the Human Body Attributed to Muʿin al-Din Chishti

Translator's Introduction

by Carl Ernst

One of the most intriguing aspects of the development of Sufism in South Asia has been the interaction of Sufis with the spiritual traditions of India, especially Yoga.[1] This short Persian text on Yoga and meditation is attributed to the famous founder of the Indian Chishti Sufi order, Shaykh Mu'in al-Din Chishti (d. 1236). A number of different versions of this treatise exist often with different titles, though most commonly it is called the *Treatise on the Human Body* (*Risala-i Wujudiyya*).[2]

---

1. For an overview of the issues surrounding the relationship of Sufism and Yoga, see Carl Ernst, "Situating Sufism and Yoga," *Journal of the Royal Asiatic Society,* Series 3, 15:1 (2005), pp. 15-43; and "The Islamization of Yoga in the *Amrtakunda* Translations," *Journal of the Royal Asiatic Society,* Series 3, 13:2 (2003), pp. 199-226.

2. Muslim philosophers interpret the key term in the title (*Wujūd*) as the abstract concept of existence, but it also has an archaic meaning of "body" and it is systematically treated in that way in this text. Manuscripts of this text are found as 6314 Ganj Bakhsh, Islamabad, entitled simply *Treatise of Mu'in al-Din Chishti*; cited by Ghulam-'Ali Arya, *Tariqa-i Chishtiyya dar Hind wa Pakistan* (Tehran: Kitabfurushi-i Zavvar, 1365/1987), p. 100. And also *Treatise on Horizons and Souls* (*Risala-i Afaq wa Anfus*), 1754 India Office Library, London, fols. 272–74; and the *Treatise on Spiritual Cultivation about of the Channels of the Human Being* (*Risala dar suluk dar sha'n-i ragha-yi adami*), MS 152 Pir Muhammadshah Dargah, Ahmedabad, fols. 1-15. There are at least nine other MSS in libraries in Pakistan, of which the two oldest are dated 1084/1673; for details, see Ahmad Munzavi, *Fihrist-i mushtarak-i nuskha-ha-yi khatti-i farsi-i Pakistan* (Islamabad: Markaz-i Tahqiqat-i Farsi-i Iran u Pakistan, 1363/1405/1985), 3:2101-3, no. 3820.

This text on Yoga and cosmology is attributed to Muʿin al-Din Chishti but this is probably fictional. The successors of Muʿin al-Din asserted that he never wrote anything. No manuscript of this text is older than the late seventeenth century. Why should such a collection of teachings with Indic psychophysical practices be attributed to Muʿin al-Din Chishti? In one sense, this attribution is an indication of the seriousness with which Indian Sufis approached the meditation practices of Yoga. These teachings were important enough that they should have been part of the teaching of the greatest Sufi master in the Chishti tradition.

The text is divided into three short chapters. Chapter 1 begins abruptly, omitting the customary praise of God and the Prophet Muhammad, and it consists of an account of the subtle physiology of Hatha Yoga, with emphasis on the three channels that parallel the spinal column.[3] It relates in detail an esoteric system of breath control related to a complicated cosmology, which assumes the concept of the human body as the microcosm related to the larger universe as macrocosm. Many details are obscure and demand more explanation than the text provides, which presumably would be available from oral commentary by a master. Chapter 2 carries forward the microcosm-macrocosm analogy with frequent quotations from the Qurʾan. Chapter 3 has an interestingly composite structure, in which the metaphysical levels and archangels of Islamic cosmology are linked to the breaths of Yogic practice.

The text asserts that the realization of these levels is closely related to the supreme spiritual states associated with the Prophet Muhammad, especially with knowledge revealed during his ascension to heaven (*miʿraj*). Moreover it maintains

3. For detailed accounts of these Yogic teachings, see Mircea Eliade, *Yoga: Immortality and Freedom,* trans. Willard R. Trask, Bollingen Series LVI (2nd ed., 1969); David Gordon White, *The Alchemical Body: Siddha Traditions in Medieval India* (Chicago: The University of Chicago Press, 1996); George Weston Briggs, *Gorakhnath and the Kanphata Yogis* (Calcutta, 1938; reprint ed., Delhi: Motilal Banarsidass, 1980).

that this knowledge was then conferred on Muʿin al-Din Chishti, either spontaneously by the Prophet Muhammad or through the agency of Muʿin al-Din's master, Shaykh ʿUthman Harwani. Muʿin al-Din is warned not to transmit this esoteric teaching to just anybody, but the restrictions are generous enough to include sincere followers of the Chishti order in later generations.

Editor's Comment

by Scott Kugle

This text is both profound and puzzling. It is known by many different titles: *Treatise: On the Human Body*, or *On World Beyond and the Soul Within*, or *On Spiritual Cultivation about the Channels in the Human Being.* It displays a deep Islamic piety rooted in certain verses of the Qur'an, and pictures this piety as compatible with Indian devotional traditions like Hatha Yoga. The text is attributed to Khwaja Mu'in al-Din Chishti. We know little about him for certain, and the lack of historically credible biographical material only fuels the loving urge to make Mu'in al-Din into a legendary spiritual hero.

Surely, for innumerable Muslims in South Asia—both for those belonging to the Chishti lineage and for almost all other Sufis as well—Mu'in al-Din is a legendary saint who radiates spiritual power and under whose protection falls the whole of South Asia. To Mu'in al-Din, tradition ascribes certain texts. Since the medieval period, these writings are assumed by Chishti Sufis to accurately convey the personality and teachings of Mu'in al-Din. Yet in all likelihood, the attribution to Mu'in al-Din is false. The earliest sources from the Chishti lineage assert that Mu'in al-Din and his immediate successors wrote no texts.

Like these other texts, the *Treatise on the Human Body* is also attributed to Khwaja Mu'in al-Din. How are we to understand that attribution? Carl Ernst has rightly pointed out that this text was not written by Shaykh Mu'in al-Din Chishti, yet all the manuscripts of this text are attributed to him. Are we to conclude that their attribution of authorship to Muʿin al-Din is simply a lie, though one made persuasive by repetition? Perhaps the question is too narrowly framed.

Before making a judgment about authorship of a text, it is necessary to investigate what kind of text it is. Not all texts have single authors in the way that modern readers may assume. For instance, we know that E. M. Forster wrote *A Passage to India,* and so it would be a lie to assert that it was written by Salman Rushdie. But not all texts are like modern novels. Devotional texts, in particular, may not have single authors. They may be the product of many generations of accumulation of text, with commentary and clarification. It might be said that such texts are authored by a "tradition" rather than by a single person.[1] In this sense, the attribution of this *Treatise on the Human Body* to Muʿin al-Din is more symbolic than actual; it signals that the text emerged from the collective experience of many generations of Chishti Sufi devotees. Just as these Sufis take their communal name "Chishti" from the saint whom they consider the "founder" of their spiritual path, Khwaja Muʿin al-Din from Chisht, so they also attribute a document that circulated among them to convey wisdom to the authorship of Muʿin al-Din. By attributing it to Muʿin al-Din, Chishti Sufis gave it value and advocated its use as a devotional aid that expresses some of their most deeply held convictions. A historical assessment of authority might miss the deeper point of the text's nature and usefulness!

So this *Treatise on the Human Body* should not be seen as the product of one person's imagination and one man's pen. If it were the product of one person's systematic exposition, we

1. The question of authorship of this text can be compared to the question of authorship of the *Yoga Sutra*, a foundational text for Hatha Yoga that is attributed to the sage Patanjali. There is persistent doubt as to the identity of Patanjali, and the nature of the text itself allows for a composite composition that grew steadily over many generations. See Barbara Stoler Miller (trans.), *Yoga Discipline of Freedom: The Yoga Sutra attributed to Patanjali* (Berkeley: UC Press, 1996).

would judge the text to be a failure because it is so fragmentary and elusive. But if we see the text as the product of a communal effort over many generations, then we can understand its real value. The text is quite sketchy and difficult to understand. It makes reference to terms without defining them. It alludes to practices without describing them. It offers a framework for devotional practice without providing any details of how to achieve its lofty goals. This text is clearly a written companion to an elaborate oral tradition of inspiring mystical insight through disciplining the body. The bulk of that tradition would be oral, transmitted from spiritual guide to initiated disciple; this written document only provides a sketch of that tradition's aspirations, goals and foundational axioms. As a text, this treatise proves the existence of an oral tradition of devotional exercises, and it also hints at that tradition's richness and potential for inter-religious synthesis. But as a text, this treatise does not document the full content of that oral tradition, in which yogic techniques merged with Sufi contemplative discipline.

As a written text, this treatise dates only from the 17th century during the Mughal period. We have no manuscript copies that exist from a date earlier than this. Nor do we have any reference to this text in other authentic sources from an earlier period. Yet though the text might date only from the Mughal era, the core ideas might have been passed on in an oral tradition from a much earlier time. In that sense, the core ideas of the treatise probably have a much earlier origin, perhaps even with the earliest Chishti Sufi teachers in India. Seen in this perspective, the attribution to Muʿin al-Din Chishti might point to the ancestry of these ideas and practices in an oral tradition that was passed on from "bosom to bosom" from a spiritual guide to initiated disciples.

The attribution should not be interpreted literally to mean that Muʿin al-Din Chishti wrote this text himself. It might be that Muʿin al-Din and other early masters of the Chishti order in India taught certain meditation practices that were in parallel with Yogic practice or perhaps borrowed from it. We know, for instance, that there were certain dramatic parallels between Sufi concepts of physio-psychic centers in the body and similar concepts held by Yogis in India. Among Sufis in Central Asia, such an energy center was known as *latifa* or "subtle center." Among Yogis in India, it was known as *chakra* or "revolving center." Beginning with the figure of Muʿin al-Din Chishti, this Central Asian Sufi tradition came to India, and later generations of Indian Sufis sought to refine the parallel concepts held by these two traditions. They sought to harmonize these two traditions, especially through the practice of "suspending the breath," which was cultivated by Yogis in India and by Sufis in Central Asia independently. This treatise gives vivid evidence of this process, which had reached a state of maturity by the Mughal era.

Certainly, the earliest Chishti sources which give a biography of Muʿin al-Din, telling the narrative of his settling in India, include many stories of his intimate interactions with Yogis, Brahmins, and Hindu mystics. These narratives tell of Muʿin al-Din deciding to settle at Ajmer, the site of an ancient temple to the deity Brahma, who represents the creative force and cosmic soul. They mention that he studied Sanskrit in order to understand the profound religious literature of Hinduism and in order to engage in discussions with Brahmins. They also tell of his adopting Indian musical modes in order to convey an Islamic and Sufi message, giving rise over time to the distinctive use of music for meditation that characterizes the Chishti Sufi order. They also tell of his acrimonious conflict with certainly local Brahmins and Yogic adepts who resented his settling there or saw him as representing the vanguard of polluting foreigners—Muslim Turks (or *Turuksha* as they were known in Sanskrit and Indian vernaculars of the time)—who were threatening to overpower South Asia militarily.

These biographical narratives may be wholly legendary or they may carry a kernel of truth in their heroic retelling. In either case, the figure of Muʿin al-Din is important as a symbol for the encounter between Muslims and Hindus, a new chapter of which opened with his settlement in India and propagation of Sufi ideals and practices there, in a mode characterized by deep appreciation of India's spiritual and aesthetic heritage. The meeting and merging between Yogic discipline and Sufi devotion is only one aspect of Muʿin al-Din's legacy. The *Treatise on the Human Body* deserves to be read, translated and studied to understand this convergence of two ancient wisdom traditions. It may even inspire readers to take up the practice of Sufi meditation or Yogic exercise, or to explore the commonalities between these two.

There is yet another reason to read this text, and that reason becomes significant when it is coupled with the other Sufi meditation texts in this volume. This text offers perhaps the earliest mention of two key concepts in the Chishti Sufi meditation tradition: the "Praised Station" (*maqam mahmud*) and the "Helping Authority" (*sultan nasir*). These terms were extracted from the Qurʾan and refined to refer to psycho-spiritual states of a person ecstatic in meditation. A sequence of two verses in the Qurʾan mentions two spiritual states—a "Praised Station" and an "Aiding Authority"—that are causal forces in transforming a devotee's late-night prayers and meditation vigils into a positive experience of rapture and ascension. The whole verse reads: "Pray in the late stretches of the night an additional voluntary prayer, that your Lord might send you to a praised station. Say, 'Oh my Lord, make my entering by the entryway of sincerity and make my leaving by the exit of sincerity and let me receive from you an aiding authority!'"[2] This treatise gives the earliest evidence that these two terms were being used to guide meditation practices in the Chishti Sufi order.

2. Surat al-Isra 17:79-80.

Yet the meaning of these terms is very allusive. These two terms helped Chishti Sufis to refine their experiences of ecstatic bliss, and to understand how this monistic union with pure being was to be reconciled with Islamic scriptural norms. These terms appear to be a distinctively Chishti contribution to Sufi meditation in general. The earliest texts by Qadiri Sufis in South Asia do not seem to use these terms; for example, *The Compass of Truth* written by Dara Shikoh does not mention these terms. Yet later meditation manuals, like *The Alms Bowl of Shaykh Kalimullah,* who had initiation into both the Chishti and Qadiri orders, do use these terms. In fact, Shaykh Kalimullah describes a distinct meditation practice guided by these two terms. Though the terms are slightly garbled: both are called stations (*maqam*)—the "Praised Station" and the "Station of Aid" (whereas in the Qur'an the second one is the "Aiding Authority"). Yet Shaykh Kalimullah leaves no doubt that these two terms are linked to the same practice, for he specifies that it also uses the technique of focusing both eyes on the tip of the nose or between the eyebrows ("Chapter 2 Morsel 12"). It appears as if this were the same practice alluded to in this *Treatise on the Human Body* attributed to Muʿin al-Din Chishti. It appears that the authors of the *Treatise on the Human Body* and the author of *The Alms Bowl* were drawing off of a common tradition of oral teaching that featured these two terms. The technical vocabulary might vary from one generation to the next or from one teaching circle to the next, but the actual practice as a ritual remains fairly constant.

This treatise attributed to Muʿin al-Din Chishti has many parallels with Hatha Yoga texts in its basic religious presuppositions, its technical understanding of anatomy, and in its prescriptive meditation practices. A good comparison is to the *Shiva Samhita,* a Sanskrit text on Hatha Yoga mentioned earlier. *The Shiva Samhita* was written as a compilation of advice on the nature of God, the human body, and how it can be harnessed to realize union with the divine; its subject and style are directly comparable to the *Treatise*. The *Shiva Samhita* is attributed to a single author, the deity Shiva, but is obviously a composite that evolved over many generations with numerous variations based on practice and oral advice. This textual structure is also comparable to the *Treatise* which, though attributed to a respected ancient source—Muʿin al-Din Chishti—is most likely a later written record of oral teachings that evolved in practice over many generations. Finally, the text of *Shiva Samhita* can be dated to roughly 1500; and the text of the *Treatise* is assumed to have been written down in the Mughal period, though in fact both texts record meditation techniques that were in practice for many centuries before.

The *Shiva Samhita* presents a monistic worldview in which there is only one absolute being—the divine being—and all appearances of diversity are illusion that must be dispelled by devoted contemplation. In the *Shiva Samhita,* God says, "The entire universe, animate and inanimate, comes from me. Everything is seen through me. Everything comes to rest in me. I am no different from it and nothing in this world is different from me. In the same way that single sun reflects innumerable times in innumerable bowls full of water, so diversity is seen in the world. But just as there are as many suns as there are bowls, so there are as many selves as there are conditions for their appearance. Just as in a dream the dreamer appears in many different ways but is one on awakening, so the universe appears to have many forms."[3] Compare this to a Persian ghazal attributed to Muʿin al-Din Chishti.[4]

> I see the reflection of his beauty in my soul's mirror,
> just like
> I see the blazing sun reflected in a pool of pure still water

3. James Mallinson, *The Shiva Samhita,* 9-10.
4. *Divan-i Hazrat Muʿin al-Din Chishti* (Lithograph; Lucknow: Munshi Nawal Kishore Press), 48. Its first couplet is "*Andar aʾina-yi jan ʿaks-i jamali deedam / ham-chu khursheed keh dar ab-i zulali deedam.*"

The gaze of reason is stunned by one ray of
  my beloved's face
I see his image despite the obscuring of a hundred veils

The light shining from my soul's mirror is of the essence
I see it, however, as a metaphor representing the truth

Let me be excused for acting so bewildered and drunk
I see his beauty and goodness in my amazement's mirror

I am a drunken lover since I heard "Am I not your Lord?"
I see reason and intelligence as impossible for me

My being is gone and all that's left is his absolute being
I see all this as exile endured in hopes of some future union

Through a painful narrowness I've entered the party
  of oneness
I see nothing as impossible after passing through
  such an ordeal

In the expanse of "all is he" this whole world and cosmos
I see as less than a crowing cock unable to even fly

Since Muʿin left phenomena's dust for eternity's light
I see no impending dawn and no sunset and no high noon

This poem cites the Qurʾanic phrase "Am I not your Lord?" to denote the moment when God faced all human beings directly, in the spiritual world before their material manifestation, and asked "Am I not your Lord?"[5] This is the moment called "the primordial covenant." It forms one of the basic concept of Sufism: all human beings have shared the intimacy of God's presence and have born witness to God's lordship before their creation, and each must now strive to remember the resonance of that moment, which forms the basis of faith. This remembrance is the goal of the ritual of zikr or meditation, which forms the basic subject of all the texts translated in this book.

5. Surat al-Aʿraf 7:172. See Carl Ernst, *Sufism: The Shambhala Guide* (Boston: Shambhala Publications, 1997), 184–85.

Although the content of this treatise alludes to commonalities with the Hatha Yoga tradition, and elements of Hinduism in general, it is allusive. This translation presents an almost untranslatable text. Some passages are quite cryptic. Others are nearly illegible. Others represent sounds in Sanskrit through the letters of the Arabic alphabet, rendered by scribes who probably did not know Sanskrit! The challenges to a translator are quite formidable. Carl Ernst has ventured boldly where few dare to tread. He had originally published side-by-side translations of two variations of this text that he had on hand.[6] This is sound scholarly practice, as it preserves the differences so that the reader can compare and come to her or his own conclusion. As the editor, I have adapted his bold scholarly translation and made it even more audacious. I have taken two more variations of the text that I have on hand, compared them to the two that Carl Ernst had originally translated, and endeavored to synthesize their variations into a single text. This is not very sound scholarly practice! But as an editor, I found that the gaps in one variation of the text were often filled in by other copies, such that a composite picture of the text's intent emerged from a comparison of several variations of it, each of which is by itself incomplete.

To create this synthesis, I have taken the liberty of altering some passages of the scholarly translation offered by Carl Ernst, with many apologies to him. Yet I freely admit the resulting synthesis contains mainly the original translation's words, with many thanks to him. It is hoped that the resulting synthesis will be useful to general readers and spiritual seekers, who care more for the enduring intent of the text than for a literal exposition of its difficulties. It is also hoped that scholars who read this synthesis translation will be lenient with the editor who oversaw its hodge-podge birth, and will acknowledge that

6. Carl Ernst, "Two Versions of a Sufi Text on Yoga and Cosmology Attributed to Shaykh Mu'in al-Din Chishti," *Elixir* 2: 69-77.

the intent of this synthesis is to affirm the text's importance and offer an approximation of its meaning rather than to give a definitive edition or literal translation.

Treatise on the Human Body Attributed to Khwaja Mu'in al-Din Chishti

In the name of God, the compassionate and merciful. Oh Lord, make the way easy for us and lead us to a good end!

This is a treatise in which I explain the knowledge and spiritual training of the Yogis, as they are known in the Indian language.

Chapter 1

Know that in the human being the first thing that appeared was the channel called *sukhumnā*.[1] Then came the channels called *ingalā* and *pingalā*. From these three, the nine channels became manifest and from these nine, the 360 channels and the 16,000 came into existence. But the goal of these is the three channels, and their root is the one called *sukhumnā*.[2]

1. Sanskrit term sometimes transliterated *sushumna*. Meditation by activating this channel is an ancient idea in India. In the Maitri Upanishad, it is written, "There is a channel called the Susumna, leading upward, conveying the breath, piercing through the palate. Through it, by joining the breath, the syllable *Aum* and the mind, one may go aloft. Beck, *Sonic Theology*, 46.
2. These are channels (*rag* in Persian, *nadi* in Sanskrit) in the body that convey energy and give life. Carl Ernst had translated the Persian term *rag* as "vein." This is technically correct, as the term does denote a blood vessel (either vein or artery) in anatomical texts. But this translation prefers to render the term as "channel" because in this text (as in the Hatha Yoga tradition as a whole) these are channels that convey energy (sometimes described as "breath") through the body; they do not refer specifically to channels that circulate blood, as implied by the word vein. For example, James Mallinson, *The Shiva Samhita*, 33, writes that a *nadi* or channel conveys sensations and conduct the winds across and along the body; this cannot refer to veins and arteries as understood through anatomy.

The *sukhumnā* channel draws the breath from below the navel, and its root is at the center below the genitals.[3] From there it rises upward. The *ingalā* and *pingalā* are the channels of the left and right of the *sukhumnā.* Whenever the seeker draws breath from the navel, it is through the *sukhumnā*. Then it comes to the heart. From that place, it divides in three parts, and going among flesh, skin, and arteries, it enters into the head. Then, going out between the two eyebrows, it comes to its place and circles three times. When the seeker wishes to suspend his breath and to become aware of its substance, he closes the nine doorways (nine orifices of the body) and he eats mild and scanty food. Then during a forty-day retreat, a knot appears beneath the breast; in the second retreat, it is at the waist; and in the third retreat—if the seeker takes on very difficult austerities and eats less and concentrates greatly—the knot appears above. When this knot is firmly established, vision and wisdom of the three knots is firmly established. Then the breath is within and it circles there three times.

Then he goes with the breath by the way of the mother's womb. There are six doorways there, within the folds of the navel in the midst of the knot of the throne, which has three doorways on the right side, and three doorways on the left side. Having opened these six doorways, he enters the window of the loins (*rozan-i sulb* or lumbar window). There he travels through twenty-eight stations. In each direction there are four foundations (*rukn*) and there are twenty-eight stations. First,

3. The Persian word for navel is *naf*; it means the region within the abdomen more than the actual navel of skin on the surface of the body. The word for genitals is *alat* (in Persian an abridgement of the more formal Arabic *alat al-tanassul* or "organ of procreation"). There is some confusion in various copies of the manuscript about this word *alat*; the Pir Muhammad Shah manuscript is clear in stating that this channel is "at the center below the genitals" (*bikh-i sukhumna dar miyan dar zer-i alat ast*), which conforms also with Hatha Yoga teaching that this energy channel is rooted in the *muladhara* or subtle energy center at the body's base "two fingers (width) above the anus and two fingers below the penis and four fingers broad and flat"; see Mallinson, *The Shiva Samhita,* 31.

the seeker wants these twenty-eight stations, and at each station is a spiritual guardian (*muwakkal*). He recognizes them, for their origin is from five things. From among them, four are of a dominant quality and one is of a dependent quality. He takes them as guides (*murshid*) in his affairs, though in fact they are of him and are from his reality (*haqiqat-i khud*). From those five people, twenty-eight people appear with these details to their appearance: five are of earth and their color is yellow, five are of water and their color is white, eight of them are of air and their color is green, five are from fire and their color is red, and five are from light and their color is black.

These twenty-eight stations are the cycle of the moon (*da᾿irat-i mahtab*). There are twenty-eight stations of increasing (*᾿uruj*) and they are the stations of the right. There are twenty-eight of diminishing (*nuzul*) and they are the stations of the left. Those twenty-eight stations have three knots and three whirlpools (*gird-ab*). There the breath becomes three lotuses (*bāraj*).

At that time, this sign appears. First, as he draws in a breath and (holds it) within, in a week he takes in five (breaths) from the stomach, and the stomach is set right. The sign that the stomach is set right is that whatever he may eat gets consumed, but if he does not eat he does not desire food and yet much power appears in him. After the stomach is set right, it (the breath) goes between the flesh, skin, and blood to the extent that for one week it goes between them. In every inhalation of breath, three times each it goes between them. At that time, the flesh and blood decrease. The sign of that is that whatever secret is hidden appears to him. Spiritual disclosure (*kashf*) appears. Then the seeker reaches perfection.

Chapter 2

When God desired, "I want to make my own divinity manifest openly that I might witness myself," then God caused creation from nonexistence the four elements (*'anasir*) and four realms of being (*wujud*) and four souls (*nafs*).[4] In this way creation happened when God desired to openly manifest the hidden secret of God's own divinity.

What did God do? First, God manifested from God's own pure essence a light (*nur*). It emerged from the divine essence in a single point and became established in four levels: the realm of divinity (*lāhūt*), the realm of archetypes (*jabarūt*), the angelic realm (*malakūt*), and the human realm (*nāsūt*), just like fire, air, water, and earth. In this way each became established as separate from God with four foundations (*rukn*). And likewise, the elements (*taba'i*) are four. And likewise, the archangels (*farishta muqarrib*) are four. And likewise, the intimate friends who supported our Prophet Muhammad—may God praise and bless him—are four.[5]

In this way from a single point creation emerged. And likewise, the human soul is of four kinds: the soul that incites to evil (*al-nafs al-ammāra*), the soul that blames (*al-nafs al-lawwāma*), the inspired soul (*al-nafs al-mulhama*), and the tranquil soul (*al-nafs al-mutma'inna*).[6] They are of four kinds, just as there are four elements: air is related to the spirit, water is related to the intellect, fire is related to love, and earth is related to the soul. Even so, the soul that incites to evil is related to fire, the

4. There is some ambiguity in the manuscripts about whether this word is "four souls" or "four breaths." This is because the word for soul (nafs) and breath (nafas) appear the same written in Persian when no vowel signs are specified. This translation favors "souls" because the four kinds of soul are detailed one paragraph later; however, in Chapter 3 the text describes four kinds of breath.

5. The phrase *chahar yar-i ghar* means the "four friends of the cave." These are the four friends who helped Muhammad ('Ali, Abu Bakr, 'Umar and 'Uthman) especially in the crisis of his exile from Mecca and escape to Medina when he had to hide in a cave (*ghar*).

6. It is a foundational idea in Sufism that the state of the soul can progress through four levels in reference to the Qur'an: the soul that incites to evil (Surat Yusuf 12:53)), the soul that blames (Surat al-Qiyamat 75:2), the inspired soul (Surat al-Shams 91:8), and the tranquil soul (Surat al-Fajr 89:27).

soul that blames is related to water, the inspired soul is related to air, and the tranquil soul is related to earth.

God has created the cosmos such that everything in the external world (*afaq*) is also created likewise in human existence (*wujud-i insan*). This is in accord with the divine word: "We shall show them our signs on the horizons and in your souls; do you not then have insight?"[7] In this way God created twelve zodiacal signs in heaven and has also created their correspondence in the human being. First, the head is Aries, Taurus is the shoulders, Gemini the hands, Cancer the arm, Leo the breast, Virgo the belly, Libra the navel, Scorpio the genitals, Sagittarius the thigh, Capricorn the leg, Aquarius the shank, and Pisces the sole of the foot. And the seven planets that wander through these twelve zodiacal signs correspond as follows: the Sun is the heart, Jupiter the liver, the Moon the lungs (*shush*), Mercury the kidney (*gurda*), Saturn the spleen (*supurz*), Mars the brain, and Venus the gall bladder (*zahra*).

In this same way God divided the year into 360 days, and also created the human being in 360 degrees. The zodiacal signs of the heavens cover 360 degrees, and on the face of the earth there are 360 mountains and 360 great rivers. In the human being, 360 individual bones stand in the place of mountains and 360 veins in the place of the rivers. 360 pieces of flesh are in place of the 360 degrees of the zodiac, and 360 pieces of skin in place of the days.

The belly of a man is like the sea, and the hair is like trees, and in the forest and meadow there are biting worms and the like; and genital worms are in that position. The face is like an inhabited building. The back is like a desert and wasteland. In the world there are four seasons, and in the human such as these exist: childhood is spring, youth is summer, maturity is a fall, and old age is the rainy season.

7. This phrase combines two verses from the Qur'an which both say "and in our souls" (Surat al-Fusilat 41:53 and Surat al-Dhariyat 51:21).

Corresponding to thunder is the human voice, to lightning is laughter, and to rain is crying. Know that the ear drinks water from the bladder, and because of that its water is bitter (*talkh*). The eye drinks water from the liver, and because of that, its water is salty (*shor*). The nose drinks water from the lungs, and therefore its water is (sour?). The tongue drinks water from the heart, and its water is sweet (*shirin*). Reason (*ʿaql*) is in the head (*dimagh*), modesty in the eye (*chashm*), understanding is in the ear (*gosh*), knowledge in the breast (*sina*), and thought is in the heart (*dil* or *qalb*).[8]

The divine creator brought the cosmos into being with seven levels to the heaven and seven levels to the land, as in the verse of Qurʾan, "We arranged one level upon another."[9] First is the heaven of Saturn, second the heaven of Jupiter, third the heaven of Mars, fourth the heaven of the Sun, fifth the heaven of Venus, sixth the heaven of Mercury, seventh the heaven of the Moon. And these correspond to the seven veils (*parda*) in the human being. The creator of the cosmos made four witnesses (*shahid* or *guwah*) in fire, air, water, and earth.

Further, from the one true reality (*haqq*) is manifested its distillation (*khulasa*) as the divine secret (*sirr*). From the divine secret is manifested its distillation as light (*nur*). From light is manifested its distillation as fire. From fire is manifested its distillation as moist atmosphere (*hawa-ab*). From atmosphere is manifested its distillation as soil (*turab*). Further, from the soil arises its essence (*zubda*) as plants. From the plants arises its essence as animals, and from animals arises its essence as humanity, and the essence of humanity is the perfect human (*insan-i kamil*). And the essence of the perfect human being is the one real true reality of God.

8. The word for head (*dimagh*) can also denote the brain or nasal cavity or region above the palate of the mouth; because of this ambiguity, this translation prefers to simply say "head" but readers should be aware of the possible nuances.

9. Surat al-Inshiqaq 84:19.

Chapter 3

My dear, you should strive to understand all I have said. Then you should know the four breaths and grow familiar with them and recognize the quantity of each of these four. What is the quantity of these four breaths, and what power does each engender? The seeker must look into this deeply and must realize it through profound introspection. That is an essential obligation (*farz ʿain*) for each person to demonstrate their realization of this before their spiritual guide (*murshid*).

Further, it is said that "Knowledge is a single point."[10] You must understand what is meant by this single point. In each principle there is a word, and in each word there is a station. The divine realm (*lahut*) is fivefold, my son. The spiritual realm (*malakut*) is the branch of that tree. The realm of divine might (*jabarut*) is the leaf, behold it. The realm of human phenomena (*nasut*) in the world is just like fruit.

The realm of divinity (*lahut*) corresponds to the tongue, the station of the Holy Spirit. The archangel Gabriel (*Jibraʾil*) knows it.[11] The place of Gabriel is "the praised station" (*maqam mahmud*).[12] Gabriel is earthy and the "praised station" is also an earthy name; its color is yellow and its taste is thick. Drawing the breath is a distance of twelve fingers beyond.[13]

---

10. In Arabic, this saying is: "*al-ʿilm nukta.*"

11. Gabriel is one of the four archangels who is also called "the holy spirit" (*al-ruh al-quds* as in Surat al-Nahl 12:103) in the Qurʾan, and Gabriel is responsible for conveying God's presence and message to humanity. Gabriel is named in the plural here (*arwah al-muqaddas*), perhaps out of respect for his greatness.

12. Surat al-Isra 17:79-80

13. The manuscript then says, "In the Indian language, it is called *mangalī mandala vartākamal lahndar.*" The text gives equivalents "in the Indian language" to these regions/angels/breaths. The Indian language appears to be Sanskrit, but the actual words are highly ambiguous and are varied in different manuscripts. Little sense can be made of these equivalents. For that reason, they are given here in the footnotes, rather than in the translation above.

The spiritual realm (*malakut*) corresponds to the nose, and its station is the navel. The archangel Israfil knows it.[14] Israfil is airy; his color is green and his taste is sour. Drawing the breath is a distance of eight fingers beyond.[15]

The realm of divine might (*jabarut*) corresponds to the eye, and its station is the top of the head. The archangel Michael knows it.[16] Michael is watery, and the station of the top (of the head) is also watery; its color is white, its form is like the form of the new moon, and its taste is sweet.[17] Drawing the breath is sixteen fingers beyond.[18]

The realm of humanity corresponds to the ear. The archangel ʿAzraʾil knows it.[19] ʿAzraʾil is fiery, and the station of the ear is also fiery. Its color is red, and its taste is bitter, and its form is like a coiled serpent (*shikanj*), and this form of a coil glows bright red like a burning lamp. Drawing the breath is a distance of four fingers beyond.[20]

That is the "helping authority" (*sultan nasir*), and the "praised station" (*maqam mahmud*), the light of divine majesty (*nur-i jalal*) and the light of divine beauty (*nur-i jamal*), the light of Muhammad and Ahmad and Mahmud and Ahad.[21]

14. Israfil is one of the four archangels, known in Christianity as Rafael. Israfil announces judgment day by blowing upon the trumpet at the end of time.
15. The manuscript then says, "In the Indian language they call this *barkamal tālī or balkamal pa.*
16. Mikha'il or Michael is one of the four archangels, who is the angel of mercy or rain, and is the sustainer of life.
17. The image of the top of the cranium being associated with the new moon and with a sweet white liquid like nectar is common to Hatha Yoga, which associates the top of the head with Shiva, the male principle of divinity, which secretes the nectar of life or *amrit* that passes down the spine to nourish life.
18. The manuscript then says, "In the Indian language they call this *shatadhal kamal barawwan hathil* or *balkamal badu*."
19. ʿAzraʾil is one of the four archangels, who is the angel of death
20. The manuscript then says, "In the Indian language they call this *madkamal amal* or *malkamal an kah*."
21. The text cites again Surat al-Isra 17:79. Here a relationship is suggested between the "praised station" and the "aiding authority." It is a praised station because it is the place or the spiritual condition in which God's aiding authority

And these are the four bodies: the subtle body (*tan-i latif*), the gross body (*tan-i kasif*), the body of annihilation (*tan-i fana*ʾ), and the body of eternality (*tan-i baqa*ʾ). These are the four spirits: the lowly spirit (*ruh-i safali*), the lofty spirit (*ruh-i* ʿ*alawi*), the holy spirit (*ruh-i qudsi*), and the angelic spirit (*ruh-i malaki*). "Truly God encompasses everything."[22]

From this you should recognize these four breaths. The quantities associated with each of them you should learn from your spiritual guide. Then you should draw them all together in as a single breath, in a particular fashion from one place of the breath to another, as is written above. You should practice this until that air (*bād*) of "the praised station" and "the aiding authority" becomes dominant. As long as the seeker does not traverse these four breaths, annihilation in the master (*fanā*ʾ *fi*ʾ*l-shaykh*) does not take place, and there is no eternality with God (*baqā*ʾ *bi*ʾ*llāh*).

One should know these four breaths and perform the action. These four airs in the human being are each like an emperor, but despite this they obey a single person. Thus they follow as one body. And this one body is the light of Muhammad, which rides all the four elements. The light of Muhammad is the light of Ahad (of the One).

The seeker should [know] that just as all was One, even so all will be again One. Thus, the being of the light of Muhammad and the light of Ahad is an acquisition (*kasb*) from this. Wayfarers on this path are given no access to the ascension without this acquisition. For it is not possible, because the spiritual guardians (*muwakkal*) are overpowering and do not allow anyone to enter as long as he has not acquired this acquisition by the will of God.

---

comes down to or into a devoted worshipper who engages in meditation.

22. Surat al-Nisa 4:108.

My dear friends, know that this is the acquisition of the revered Prophet, taught to him by Gabriel who had learned it from God. And that time when my master and savior, Lord ʿUthman Harwani (may God sanctify his conscience) had bestowed grace and kindness upon this beggar ([Muʿin al-Din Chishti]), he took my spirit to the presence of that revered Prophet. He said, "Your highness, this is a child who is worthy of succession (*khilafat*)." The revered Messenger of God gave me this much knowledge and this divine acquisition, saying, "Oh Muʿin al-Din, God most high taught this acquisition to Gabriel, and Gabriel taught it to me. The time when God wished to send his Prophet on his mission, he separated me from that place and I became united with this acquisition. The day when this practice was completed was the very time when the ascension (*miʿraj*) became my destiny. Then my prophetic mission became manifest. Oh Muʿin al-Din, now I bestow this very acquisition upon you!"

I came to this side (the world) and became occupied with this acquisition. At the time when this practice was completed I reached the height; at that moment this beggar experienced the ascension (*miʿraj*). But I was given permission to write only this much about the effect of that experience. Again I presented my case to the Revered One with a thousand entreaties and laments, and permission was granted on the condition that he stated: "Do not speak of this to every seeker and disciple, that this secret should not go from house to house; but you can speak of this secret to sincere seekers who have more or less learned the knowledge."

My dear brother, this acquisition is something to be realized. So realize through your own experience. Then go before your spiritual guide (*murshid*). Only once the guide attests that the realizations have clearly taken place for the seeker, then he authorizes this as real acquisition. He says that spirits have two forms: one lofty and the other lowly. He adds four forms in between the two forms. Again, these two forms both have a station: one is the "Praised Station" (*maqam mahmud*) and the other is the "Helping Authority" (*sultan nasir*).[23] These are of two forms: one is a traveling form and the other is a stationary one. The seeker should know the traveling form and recognize its color, as is said above, so the seeker does not make a mistake. If no mistake is made, then the traveling form reaches the stationary form, and that stationary form attains witnessing of the real One, and in that place he attains the reality of the ninety-nine names (*asma*).

The master tells the seeker to direct his gaze down to a point at the bridge of the nose (*barra*).[24] This is from the point of view that these two eyes, which they call sun and moon, and which are related to both chief channels which in the Indian language are called *ingalā* and *pingalā*, are both related to the channel of life, which in Indian language they call *sukhumna*. These two channels, called the solar and the lunar channel, run firmly along either side of the *sukhumnā* channel. By focusing thus, the seeker's own image is effaced, in the way that we showed above. In this way, one adds a form through visualization (*tasawwur*), and that is the form of the spiritual guide (*murshid*) as if seen with the external vision.

---

23. Here the two different terms from the Qur'an, the "praised station" (*maqam mahmud*) and the "aiding authority" (*sultan nasir*) are placed in an even closer relationship, such that both are described as a kind of spiritual authority (*sultan*).

24. This word *barra* is likely related to the term *arra*, which refers to the sound generated by the breath within the nose when one meditates upon the name of God (*Allah*) within the breath. The manuscript writes *barra* but this probably denotes *bi-arra* or "at the arra" meaning the nasal region. In *The Alms Bowl,* Shaykh Kalimullah refers to this as the "*arra* of the nose" and *arra* is a Persian word meaning a saw, or friction that is like the sound of a saw. In Chapter One on Methods of Meditation, in Morsel 12, Shaykh Kalimullah writes: "it may be that a sound is generated in the nose while performing this meditation. That sound is known as 'nasal sawing' (*arra-i bini*)" and the friction from this meditation through breathing generates an internal heat.

At whatever moment is specified by the spiritual guide, the gaze is raised to a place in the center above the nose. In the midst of the nose is the station of the spiritual realm (*malakut*), and in that realm are displayed forms in a thousand ways, external and internal. But one should not pay attention to the many forms it displays, but rather one should keep holding in one's visualization the form of one's spiritual guide. One should persist with this until to the visualization of the form of the master is added the form of Muhammad. Then one attains the visualization of Muhammad, and this is superimposed upon the image of one's spiritual guide. As one attains the visualization of Muhammad, one attains the visualization of Ahad (the One). Then the reality of the ninety-nine names of God becomes manifest, and those ninety-nine names are effaced in a single name. The one name exists as "A" (*alif*). It became the inhalation of "he" (*huwa*). And "he" makes its station to be M (*mīm*). And from M is N (*nūn*). And N is W. *Wa huwa arham al-rahimin*—and he is the most merciful of the merciful!

This treatise is now complete.

Glossary

A

ab: water, one of the four elements; same as *ma'* in Arabic
af'al: actions of God
afaq: far horizon, the external sensory world
akhfa': most secret inner essence of the heart
akhfa'-i akhfa': utmost secret inner essence of the heart
amanat: the trust, conferred upon humanity by God, also called *wad'iyat*
'ansur (plural *'anasir*): element
'ashiq: lover
asma': names of God's names
atish: fire, one of the four elements; same as *nar* in Arabic
awliya: saints, the friends of God
azal: eternity before time

B

bad: air or wind, one of the four elements; same as *hawa* in Arabic
badan: body
bahs: suchness, quiddity, being one and one thing only
basit: essential and simply singular in its existence
baqa' bi'llah: sustained or remaining with God
barzakh: medium or intermediary, that which forms the boundary between two things
basirat: awareness or insight
be-hoshi: absence from one's senses
be-khudi: un-self-consciousness
be-rangi: undifferentiated state of being without qualities or colors

D

dargah: shrine at the tomb of a revered Sufi
da'wat: invocations or voluntary prayer of supplication
dil-i mudawwar: heart like a perfect sphere; source of pure mind

dil-i sanubari: heart, the physical organ of flesh shaped like a pine cone
dil-i nilofari: heart, the imaginative organ shaped like a lotus blossom that is the seat and foundation of the body
dimagh: mind, located at the top of the breath; *see umm al-dimagh*

F

fana' fi'llah: obliteration, effacement or losing one's self in God
faqr: poverty, renouncing the world
farishta: angel; same as *malak* and *mala'ika* in Arabic
farz: obligatory prayer
fath: opening or conquest
fauq: above, pronouncing *illa 'llah* or "but God" from above down onto the heart
fazl: bounty, a gift given undeserved
fikr: reflection or contemplation using an abstract mental or imaginative process
futuhat: openings, disclosures of divine presence
fuyuzat: outpourings of grace

G

ghaflat: negligence, neglect and distraction
ghayb: what is beyond the senses, spiritual realities that are unseen
ghaybat: state of self-absence

H

habs-i nafas: suspension of breath; sometimes called *habs-i dam* (*dam* is a Persian word and *nafas* in an Arabic word, but both mean "breath" and both are used in Persian)
hal: spiritual state
haqiqat: true reality or spiritual reality
hasr-i nafas: restraining of breath
hayrat: bewilderment, often termed also *tahayyur*
hazrat-i insan: primordial human being, the universal archetype of the human being
huwiyat: divine truth or identity
huzur: presence of a person or of God

I

'ibadat: worship

ʿilm: knowledge that can be learned, about religion, mysticism or other discipline is termed "compound knowledge'; in contrast knowledge that is self-evident and intuitive is termed "essential knowledge"

ikhlas: sincerity

iman: true faith

ingala: energy channel in the body to the left of *sukhumna,* associated with the moon

inayat: grace

insan: human being

insan-i kamil: perfect human, a realized human who overcomes personal limitations

ʿirfan: spiritual knowledge, *see maʿrifa*

ʿishq: passionate love

islam: outer form of religion

istighfar: seeking forgiveness from God, by saying *astaghfiru ʾllaha*

istimdad: concentrating on one's spiritual master for help or *madad*

itlaq: absolute oneness

J

jabarut: realm of divine might or spiritual archetypes

jamʿ: comprehensiveness and concentration

jamʿiyat: concentration, force of will

jazb: longing, being attracted to God or pulled away by God

K

kasb: acquisition, something that is earned or learned through one's own effort

kashf: spiritual disclosure of unseen things (in Persian *kashaʾish*)

kashkul: alms bowl used by itinerant Sufis to collect daily food donations

karamat: generous gifts of God, meaning miraculous powers

khafi: inner essence hidden deep within the heart

khak: earth or dust, one of the four elements; same as *arz* or *turab* in Arabic

khalifa: vicegerent, one who holds responsibility and authority

khanaqah: building dedicated to Sufi gatherings

khannas: the tempter who dwells in the human breast

khatra: selfish or negative thought

khilafat: succession and authority; *see khalifa*
khirqa: robe or cloak, sign of a Sufi disciple taking initiation with a spiritual guide
khulasa: distillation, when something vast is reduced to something smaller that retains the nature of the vaster original and conveys its essential meaning; *see zubda*

L

lahut: divine realm
latif: subtle, a thing of spiritual nature not limited by time and space
latifa: subtle energy center in the body, similar to what Yogis call *chakra*
latifa rabbaniya: divine quality inherent in every person
lazzat: spiritual delight, bliss
lisan: tongue or speech

M

madd: drawing out, prolonging first "a" in *la ilaha* or "no god"
mahwiyat: oblivion
ma᾿iyat: duality
mujahadat: struggle, spiritual striving
majzub: a person mad with longing for God; *see jazb*
malakut: spiritual world or angelic realm
maqam: station of the spiritual path
maratib: emanations of singular divine being into multiple levels of material being
maʿrifat: spiritual knowledge
maʿshuq: beloved
miʿraj: ascension to heaven
misal: imaginative world, the realm of images accessed through spiritual imagination
muʿayyana: beholding with one's own eyes
mulk: material world
muhabbat: love
muhdath: phenomenal, created in time and space
muharaba: war, used in the sense of a spiritual struggle against the ego
muhasibat-i nafs: keeping account of one's self, its attitudes and deeds

mujahada: struggling; *see muharaba*
mukashafa: divine inspiration or revealing the unseen
muladhara: subtle energy center at the body's base
mulk: created world
muqayyad: limited, existing in a discrete form
murakkab: compound, created from elements liable to decompose, opposite of *basit*
muraqaba: contemplation
muraqqa': patched cloak worn by Sufis as a symbol of renouncing worldly concerns
murid: disciple, one who desires spiritual guidance from a master
murshid: spiritual guide
mushahada: witnessing
muwakkal: spiritual guardian, spiritual being or force assigned to carry out a task

N

naf: navel
nafas (plural *anfas*): breath
nafil (plural *nawafil*): devotion beyond what is obligatory
nafs (plural *nufus* or *anfus*): self or soul
nafs-i natiqa: the universal intellect
namaz: prayer, see *salat*
nasut: human world perceived through the senses
nisbat: relationship, with a spiritual guide or spiritual forces
nur: light

P

parda: veil or curtain, obstructions of selfish conceit that prevent spiritual awareness
pingala: energy channel in the body to the right of *sukhumna*, associated with the sun

Q

qalb: heart, the physical organ of the body

R

rabita: connection, the bond between oneself and one's spiritual guide; *see barzakh*
rabt: attachment, to a spiritual guide

rag-i kimas: the sciatic nerve
riyazat: exertion, spiritual exercises
riza᾿: contentment
rizq: sustenance
ruh: spirit

S

sahib-dil: master of heart, spiritual guide, accomplished mystic
sajjada-nashin: hereditary custodian of Sufi lineage
salat: canonical prayer
salawat: blessing Prophet Muhammad, for example saying *sala allahu ʿalayhi wa sallim*
sawt: sound, known as the un-struck sound or everlasting sound or eternal sound
sayr fi᾿llah: journey in God
sayr ila᾿llah: journey towards God
shadd: intensifying, accentuating the first syllable "i" in *illa᾿llah* or "but God"
shahadat: visible world
shahid: witness, refers to the four elements from which all in the cosmos is created
shaytan: the force of temptation
shaykh: spiritual guide
shughl: devotional exercise
sifat: qualities of God
sidq: truthfulness
silsila: Sufi order
sirr: inner heart or divine secret
sukhumna: central energy channel in the body
sunna: optional prayers that the Prophet Muhammad used to make

T

ta᾿ayyun: manifestation or individualization of being into a certain type of creation
tahajjud: late-night vigil prayer
tahlil: praising God, by saying *al-hamdu li᾿llahi*
tahqiq: realizing the truth, realization
taht: below, pronouncing *la ilaha* downward towards the left knee and then raising it

tajalli: divine self-disclosure or manifestation of the divine
takhliya: emptying, keeping the abdomen constricted
tals: erasure, being effaced; *see fana'*
tamliya: filling, keeping the abdomen distended and swelled full
tams: annihilation, being utterly wiped out; *see fana'*
tan: body; *see badan*
tanazzuh: transcendence, being unlike any other thing, opposite of *tashbih*
taqwa: God-consciousness or awareness of God
tasawwur: visualization
tasbih: glorifying God, reciting the words *subhanullah* or other words of praise
tashbih: immanence, similarity to other existing things, opposite of *tanzih*
taslim: acceptance
tauba: repentance
tawajjuh: concentration, turning one's full attention towards a single object
tawhid: bearing witness to God's oneness; *kalima al-tawhid* saying "No god but God"

U

umm al-dimagh: source of mind, place metaphorically centered at the top of the breath
uns: intimacy

W

wahdat-i wujud: "Oneness of Being," a philosophical and mystical school of thought
wahm: delusion, false concept, fancy, egoistic notion
wajd: rapture
wajib al-wajud: the necessary being, a philosophical term for God
wali: saint, *see awliya*
waswasa: temptation
wilayat: sainthood, or power bestowed on a human being through intimacy with God
wird: litany that is chanted or read silently
wujud-i mutlaq: absolute being, an abstract conception of God
wusul: divine union

Z

zat: essence

zauq: ecstasy, spiritual appetite or refined taste for spiritual experiences

zikr: meditation using a pronounced word, phrase or breath; remembrance of God

zubda: essence, when something lesser is heated or churned to separate which is extraneous from what is purer, yet still retains the original nature of that which was lesser; *see khulasa*

Notes on the Cover Illustration

"Mu'in al-Din Chishti Holding a Globe" by Bichitr 1610-1618.

The illustration is from the collection of Dublin's Chester Beatty Library, from "The Minto Album folio 36a" CBL In 07A.14

In the image, Mu'in al-Din Chishti holds a globe symbolizing the world, surmounted by a crown of imperial rule, which holds a feather of divine favor. Written in gold inside the globe is the inscription, "The Key to the conquest of the two worlds is entrusted to your hands" (*Kalid-i fath-i do 'alam bi-dast-i tu-st musallam*). His halo of illuminated black light is symbolic of divine revelation. Written in gold against the dark green background is "by the servant of the holy court, Bichitr" (*banda-yi dargah 'amal-i bichitr*), naming the painter Bichitr, one of the most famous artists of the Mughal atelier during the reign of Jahangir.

The facing page of the album features a standing portrait of the Emperor Jahangir, painted against the same dark green background. Jahangir holds the globe that is surmounted by a key, showing that he has been handed the key of world-ruling success by the favor of God and the blessings of Mu'in al-Din Chishti.

This image was painted at Ajmer, where Jahangir was residing with the Mughal court for three years, during which time he visited the shrine (*dargah*) of Muʿin al-Din Chishti nine times and donated a golden railing to decorate his tomb.

This information is taken from Elaine Wright, Muraqqaʿ: Imperial Mughal Albums from the Chester Beatty Library (Alexandria, VA: Art Services International, 2008), pages 288-294.

Index

A

N

O

P

V

W

About the Translators

Scott Kugle is a research scholar in comparative religion and Islamic culture. He is currently Associate Professor at Emory University in Atlanta, Georgia, in the Department of Middle Eastern and South Asian Studies. His research focuses on Sufism, on devotional poetry and music, and on gender. He has lived for many years in Hyderabad, India, where he does research, occasionally teaches, and participates in the Kalimi community of the Chishti Sufi order.

Carl W. Ernst is a specialist in Islamic studies, with a focus on West and South Asia. His published research has been mainly devoted to the study of three areas: general and critical issues of Islamic studies, premodern and contemporary Sufism, and Indo-Muslim culture. On the faculty of the Department of Religious Studies at the University of North Carolina at Chapel Hill since 1992, he has been department chair and Zachary Smith Professor as well as member of the Board of Directors of the Middle East Studies Association. He is now William R. Kenan, Jr., Distinguished Professor and Co-Director of the Carolina Center for the Study of the Middle East and Muslim Civilizations.

Sulūk Press is an independent publisher dedicated to issuing works of spirituality and cultural moment, with a focus on Sufism, in particular, the works of Hazrat Inayat Khan and his successors. To learn more about Inayatiyya Sufism, please visit **inayatiyya.org**.

www.ingramcontent.com/pod-product-compliance
Lightning Source LLC
Chambersburg PA
CBHW020316080326
40747CB00001B/66

9780930872908